W9-DAW-910

NICK MURRAY

BEHAVIORAL INVESTMENT COUNSELING

The Nick Murray Company, Inc.
www.nickmurray.com

Copyright ©2008 by Nicholas Murray.
All rights reserved.

No portion of this book may be used or reproduced in any manner whatsoever without written permission. The information in this publication does not constitute a recommendation for the purchase or sale of any securities. The author is not engaged in rendering investment advisory, legal or accounting services. If such assistance is required, seek the advice of a professional.

Printed in the United States of America
Library of Congress Control Number: pns61886
ISBN: 978-0-615-25209-4

This book is for my grandchildren

REBECCA AND WILL DICKERSON

who taught me that I was born to be 'Pa

"IT WON'T BE THE ECONOMY THAT WILL DO IN INVESTORS; IT WILL BE INVESTORS THEMSELVES."

—WARREN BUFFETT

"THE INVESTOR'S CHIEF PROBLEM—AND EVEN HIS WORST ENEMY—IS LIKELY TO BE HIMSELF."

—BENJAMIN GRAHAM

"WE HAVE MET THE ENEMY, AND HE IS US."

—POGO POSSUM

TABLE OF CONTENTS

BOOK ONE
BEHAVIOR MODIFICATION AS THE ADVISOR'S VALUE

BOOK TWO
THE BEHAVIORAL APPROACH TO
SUPERIOR LIFETIME RETURNS

BOOK THREE
THE BEHAVIORAL CONVERSATION

BOOK FOUR
BEHAVIORAL COUNSEL IN SEASONS OF CRISIS

AUTHOR'S PREFACE

＿＿＿＿

THIS IS A BOOK FOR FINANCIAL ADVISORS ABOUT portfolio management. Its aims are twofold.

First, it identifies, and completely explains, a method of managing investment portfolios *primarily by managing the behavior of the owners of those portfolios*—in such a way that one's clients will consistently achieve superior long-term, real-life returns *compared to the returns realized by other investors*.

Second, this book gives the financial advisor a practice management paradigm in which he or she can deliver these consistently superior long-term, real-life returns with minimal expenditure of time and effort, and with virtually no stress.

To the harried advisor, this second aim of *Behavioral Investment Counseling* ought to be every bit as important as the first. That's because, even for the most diligent and disciplined practitioners, portfolio management seems to become not a complement to sound long-term planning, but its most vexing distraction. From the client's standpoint, a lifetime and even multigenerational planning perspective is constantly being undermined by the peregrinations of the economy, the gyrations of the markets, and the utter randomness of quarter-to-quarter "performance" comparisons.

And from the perspective of the planner herself, the time-and-energy compartments of planning and portfolio management prove, in the real world, to be anything but watertight. We all set out to devote ourselves primarily to the higher function of planning, keeping portfolio management in the subsidiary role of a tool—a means to the end of the client's goals.

But then there comes a financial "crisis," a sudden downdraft in the markets, or simply a client bleating about the shoot-the-lights-out "performance" of some manager he saw on CNBC, and we're driven completely off course. Like Frankenstein's monster, portfolio management—created only to serve a higher good—goes mad, and starts wrecking our financial planning practice.

I promise that you will find, at the end of this book, that virtually all of the hours and energy that are currently being sucked down into the black hole of portfolio management have been permanently freed up, so that you can invest them in the infinitely more productive pursuits of client acquisition and retention, fundamental financial and estate planning, continuing education, and a higher quality of life for you and the people you love.

I promise further that—provided only that you never stop prospecting for clients who have the eyes to see and the ears to hear the sublime truth of a behavioral investment philosophy—your practice will become, over time, practically free of stress. You will have no clients you don't like—or at least respect—and none who don't like, or at least respect, you.

Your clients will be largely insusceptible to volatile markets and scare headlines. They will require relatively little maintenance or handholding, since they will understand the long-term nature of the voyage upon which you and they have embarked together.

Perhaps even more wonderful and rare, they will understand *you.*

Understanding, respecting and ultimately liking you as much as they come to do, your clients will also become—perhaps with just a bit of encouragement—consistent sources of referral and introduction to other kindred souls. To the point where, one fine day, your Ark will be full, and you can gently pull up the gangplank, and sail away to the Promised Land.

It is not enough to want such a rich, remunerative and joyful professional life. You have to deserve it. All his life, George Washington was fond of quoting a line from Joseph Addison's play *Cato,* to the effect that we cannot insure success but we can deserve it. I would go beyond that, and say that the kind of success I describe in this book is available to anyone who elects to deserve it, and never to stop deserving it.

If you believe the inarguable truths advanced in this book—the essential, human, behavioral truths—and you never cease to advocate for them with passion and conviction, you will not merely *deserve* the success I describe, but you will surely *achieve* that success. It cannot be denied you. You just have to tell these truths to enough people.

I neither know nor care how many people that is. Wisdom, and the inevitability of success, will come to you when you don't care, either: when you just keep telling this story, if for nothing more than the sheer joy of telling it. John F. Kennedy defined joy as the use of all one's talents in the pursuit of excellence. This is precisely the joy I wish you.

—NICK MURRAY

INTRODUCTION

THE DOMINANT DETERMINANT OF LONG-TERM, real-life investment returns is the behavior of the investor himself.

Note the choice of the adjective *dominant*, because it is not casual, but critical. I did not suggest, for example, that behavior is the predominant determinant, since that would merely have meant that it is more important than any other single determinant. I said—and now say again—that behavior is **dominant: *it is more important than all the other determinants put together.***

Pause for a moment, here, and begin to absorb the implications of this deeply countercultural truth. Because your career, and the success or failure of your clients' long-term financial plans, depend on your willingness and ability to accept it.

Embracing this epiphany, you would put the huge preponderance of your investment management effort into inculcating and maintaining healthy behavior in your clients, and relatively little effort into managing the standard deviation of their investments. By the same logic, knowing this behavioral truth, the client would put most of his effort into making sure he was thinking clearly and behaving appropriately about his investments—rather than trying to figure out if there was going to be a recession, or parsing the latest reports on wage and productivity growth, or comparing the three year performance of all the five-star small cap value funds.

Long-term, real-life portfolio returns—the actual results that real people really get, in practice—are only marginally affected by the relative performance of investments. Rather, *they are absolutely driven by the behavior of investors.*

By and large, our clients do not think this way. Far worse, to their own sorrow, most financial advisors do not help their clients and prospects to think this way. We live in a timing and selection culture—one which holds that timing (when to be in and out of the markets, and when to move among different market sectors) and selection (which stocks, or which of several similar funds/managers, to be in) are the critical variables.

The timing and selection culture is, for all intents and purposes, a conspiracy. It isn't an active nor even a conscious conspiracy: the heads of all the major mutual fund families have not met secretly with the editors of *Money, Worth* and *Kiplinger's* magazines, the program directors of CNBC and Fox Business News, and the good people of Morningstar. (At least I don't think they have.) It's just that these businesses—and let us never forget that they are all businesses, attempting to sell something for a profit—have independently arrived at the same conclusion: that their business goals are best served by implicitly suggesting the primacy of selection and timing.

Morningstar constantly (and correctly) stresses that its star system is only a shorthand synopsis—a snapshot, if you will—of the inner workings of mutual funds. It repeats almost ritually that investors should research funds in a far deeper and more nuanced way than just counting stars. *But it does not stop publishing star ratings,* upon which, in a very real way, its business has been built.

The senior managers of the major mutual fund families all know that investors will be best served by making a financial plan, funding it with a diverse selection of quality investments, and then investing steadily in those portfolios for an entire working lifetime. No major mutual fund family is, as I write, using these essential truths as the cornerstone of its marketing and advertising. Instead, they advertise **how many of their funds carry four- and five-star ratings,** or have beaten the S&P 500—or their Lipper peer group averages—over three, five and ten year periods.

Money magazine has never had a cover story about the Brinson study—the seminal research finding that over 90% of institutional portfolios' long-term variance from their indexes has been attributable to asset allocation, with selection, timing and all other variables accounting for less than 10%. Instead, it has, on an average of once a year, run cover stories whose headlines might be summed up as "Six Hot Funds To Buy Now!"

CNBC interviews, on an average business day, a dozen talking heads, in pairs: one is a bull and the other a bear; one thinks oil will go up and the other that it will fall; ditto gold and the dollar, employment/unemployment, the dollar vs. the euro, the balance of payments deficit, growth vs. value, big cap vs. small cap, **ad infinitum, ad nauseam.** To my knowledge, it has never devoted even a quarter hour to saying: in the long run, your family's financial well-being in later life, and its ability to leave significant legacies to its children, will depend largely on what percentage of its income it manages to save—perhaps the ultimate behavioral variable.

All of these choices represent rational business decisions—indeed, in the largest sense, they are the same business decision—on the part of all these business entities. Unfortunately, that decision tends to confirm in the investor's mind a fundamental untruth: that timing and selection—which particular investments to be in, and when to be in them—are the key determinants of financial success. They are not. **Behavior is.**

All financial advisors who have imbibed the Kool-Aid of the selection and timing culture—or who are consciously and cynically giving it back to people because they know it's what prospects will buy—are witting or unwitting co-conspirators in the propagation of the same untruth. The advisor who stands up for the primacy of behavior—and who therefore espouses an almost purely behavioral value proposition—must accept that, like all essential truth tellers, he is going to be "selling" a philosophy that is still deeply countercultural.

So be it. Let the rabble compete with each other to sell investors ever more grotesque permutations of the untruth ("I can consistently pick top-performing funds, and get you consistently superior investment performance"). You will never be the most persuasive purveyor of the untruth, nor the low-cost producer of it. And you don't want to be.

You want to be out there, selling not just a great truth but *the* great truth about successful investing. You want a healthy, growing practice built on proven principles for producing consistently superior real-life returns. You want a stress-free practice which cannot be taken hostage by headlines. You want clients who are happy with you because you make them better than they are, and thereby help them achieve their most cherished financial goals. You want a practice that becomes a referral machine. ***You want to be someone that clients can believe, and believe in.***

You want, finally, to be able to say proudly what few advisors have ever dared to suggest:

"I DON'T SAY THAT THE INVESTMENTS I RECOMMEND WILL 'OUTPERFORM' MOST OF YOUR NEIGHBORS' INVESTMENTS.

"I SAY THAT, USING THE PRINCIPLES I PRACTICE, YOU SHOULD END UP WITH A FAR BETTER LIFETIME RETURN THAN DO MOST OF YOUR NEIGHBORS.

"SEEING THAT THESE ARE TWO DIF- FERENT THINGS, AND WHY THEY'RE TWO DIFFERENT THINGS, IS THE BE- GINNING OF WISDOM—AND THE BE- GINNING OF AN UNDERSTANDING OF WHAT I DO."

BOOK ONE

BEHAVIOR MODIFICATION AS THE ADVISOR'S VALUE

1

BEHAVIOR MODIFICATION
VS. PORTFOLIO MANAGEMENT

YOU CAN, ALMOST AT WILL, BECOME AN EXTRA-ordinarily effective manager of the behavior of your clients with respect to their investment decisions. This will unfailingly lead to superior long-term, real-life returns for your clients.

Alternatively, you may—with almost limitless amounts of very hard work and constant anxiety—become a relatively good manager of investment portfolios themselves. Regardless of how much time and energy you invest in this latter quest, however, you will only intermit-tently—and quite unpredictably—"outperform" the markets. And, at the end of the day, all your hard work will be destroyed by the irratio-nal behavior of your clients—speculative euphoria at market tops, and panicky capitulation at market bottoms, to name only two.

It's a choice. You must elect to pursue excellence in one area or the other. You cannot do both.

Most of the retail financial advisory profession has, consciously or unconsciously, chosen the latter course. Which is why—almost by definition—most financial advisors are mediocrities: overworked, underpaid, and chronically stressed out by the volatility of markets, by the seeming randomness of "performance," and by the sniping of "clients" whom they do not particularly like, and who do not particularly like them.

Let us examine—and attempt, however anecdotally, to quantify—the critical importance of behavior in determining real-life, long-term returns. We will find it to be very great. Then let us establish what we can know about the efficacy of—and the return on—portfolio management. We will find it to be unpredictable, uncontrollable, and largely irrelevant to real-life client outcomes. (We will also discover that portfolio management is subject to an iron law of diminishing returns to the advisor: past a certain point—and that point sets in very early—incremental expenditures of time and energy yield smaller and smaller incremental returns to the portfolio.)

The simplest, most stark and to me most compelling window into the importance of behavior is the annually updated (by Lipper and DALBAR, Inc., respectively) juxtaposition of the 20-year average annual compound rate of return of the average large cap equity mutual fund in the U.S. and the average return realized by the average equity mutual fund investor. For the 20 years through 2007, these were as follows:

AVERAGE EQUITY FUND	AVERAGE EQUITY FUND INVESTOR
10.81%	4.48%

Note that these data cover all the dollars invested by all the investors in all the large cap equity funds in this country over 20 years. They aren't skewed by anything, because they can't be. By the way, although these two numbers will bounce around a lot from year to year, *the relationship between them remains eerily constant: over 20 year periods, the average fund investor consistently manages to capture much less than half of the return of the average fund.*

Thus, in a society that has made almost a secular religion out of "outperformance," the average investor is not merely underperforming the markets: *he is underperforming—to a grotesque extent—his own investments!*

What would the average investor have had to do, over these 20 years, to earn a 10.81% compound annual return? Yes, exactly: he would have had to identify (literally) the quintessentially mediocre large cap equity fund of the next 20 years. Then he would simply have had to buy it, elect dividend reinvestment, and put it in a drawer. (It would have helped, I suppose, if he could then have forgotten about it—recalling the investment only when he happened to open that particular drawer 20 years later.)

He didn't do that. He did something else—indeed, a whole lot of other things, which had three important characteristics in common: (1) they were always the wrong thing to do, and (2) they were done at the wrong time (3) for the wrong reasons.

The foregoing paragraph contains the Supreme Secret. That is, the way the average investor blew—and consistently blows—upwards of 60% of the return of the average fund over any given 20 year period is that *he behaved inappropriately.* And the funny thing is, anybody who's been a retail financial advisor for more than about three months can probably give you a complete list of what that poor boneheaded average investor did:

- He bought only funds with the hottest recent "performance."
- When those previously hot funds inevitably lagged, he switched into the next crop of red-hot recent winners. He may have done this several times.
- In October 1987, and/or October 1990, and/or August 1998, and/or October 2002, and/or October 2008—that is, at any or all of the major bottoms of the last 20 years, when equity mutual funds went into massive net liquidation—he went to cash in a panic. In the interim, around 1999, he loaded up on tech, telecom, dot.com and other avatars of a "new era."

And how did the poor, benighted average investor's advisor respond to this? Of course: he redoubled his efforts to master Modern Portfolio Theory, or to understand the French-Fama Multifactor CAPM model, or he started studying for the CIMA designation.

That's the tragedy, in a nutshell: **presented again and again with irrefutable evidence that the central problem is emotional/behavioral—that it is housed in the investor's emotions—advisors seek ever more complex intellectual/analytical remedies, on the bizarre assumption that the problem is housed in the intellect.** And after all that painful effort, what does the left-brain, "portfoliocentric" advisor find?

1. THAT "OUTPERFORMANCE" IS NEITHER A FINANCIAL GOAL NOR A FINANCIAL PLAN. An income that a client does not outlive in retirement is a financial goal. "Outperformance" is not a financial goal, nor is it a plan for achieving an income one doesn't outlive. If I "outperform" my neighbor by 300 basis points in the 20 years to retirement—a whopping margin, by anyone's reckoning—such that he runs out of money when he is 79, and I don't run out of money until I'm 84, it will not matter much when we are both sitting on a park bench at 86, without two nickels to rub together between us. The citizens of the timing-and-selection culture don't figure this out until it's too late.

A portfolio is not a plan, and the neurotic quest for "outperformance" is very often an attempt on the investor's part to avoid the pain of planning: the necessity to set goals, to figure out what those goals will cost, and to make the commitment to save—to defer gratification—enough to fund those goals, assuming reasonable rates of return over time.

"Maybe if I pick the right nanotechnology fund—and/or the right emerging markets fund, and/or the right hedge fund—I'll be able to afford to send my daughter to Duke instead of to Brooklyn College." It sounds ridiculous when you say it that way, and there's a very good reason for that: it is ridiculous. It's portfolio selection as pipe dream.

What renders the silliness almost tragic is the suicidal acceptance, and even endorsement, of it by the financial planner—who should know better, if anyone does. The advisor who becomes complicit in the substitution of portfolio composition for sound long-term planning is more than just an enabler. He's a traitor to his own profession, and even to his own values. Somewhere along in here, you have to stop and ask yourself: ***am I a planner or a prognosticator?*** You can never be neutral on this issue: you're either part of the solution, or you are most certainly part of the problem.

2. THAT "OUTPERFORMANCE" ISN'T CONSISTENTLY ACHIEVABLE, AND ESPECIALLY THAT IT CANNOT BE INFERRED FROM PAST PERFORMANCE. Some 2,500 years ago, the Greek philosopher Heraclitus wrote, "You could not step twice into the same river, for other waters are ever flowing on to you." Let me render that into modern financial English for you:

THERE IS NO STATISTICAL EVIDENCE FOR THE PERSISTENCE OF PERFORMANCE.

Simple as that. Say it loud, say it proud and put it on your office wall in big Gothic lettering: there is no statistical evidence for the persistence of performance. The Morningstar star system exists, and is as wildly popular as it is, because people simply can't stand the ambiguity that is dictated by this simple fact: based solely on past performance, future performance will be random. A portfolio of five-star funds will either outperform a portfolio of one-star funds over the next five years or it won't: ***there's no way to know in advance.***

Does this suggest that superior performing managers cannot be identified prospectively? It most assuredly does not. It simply states that future superior performance cannot be inferred scientifically from past superior performance. Once you know this, you are a butterfly, and you can never go back to being a caterpillar again. (Or you are a pickle, and you can never again be a cucumber.) You can never make believe that you don't know that future performance can't be projected from past performance. You have to stand up for this truth, or you have to lie. And you don't want to lie, because it's career—as well as moral—suicide.

3. THAT A PRACTICE BASED EVEN IMPLICITLY ON THE LIE THAT YOU CAN OPPORTUNELY AND CONSISTENTLY PREDICT OR CONTROL TIMING, SELECTION AND/OR RELATIVE PERFORMANCE IS A PRACTICE OF RENTING MONEY—A SYSTEM OF PROGRESSIVELY DISAPPOINTING ALL THE PEOPLE IN YOUR BOOK, SO THAT YOU HAVE TO BE CONSTANTLY FINDING NEW PEOPLE IMPLICITLY TO LIE TO. A lie in which we do not actually enunciate an explicit untruth—but rather give the prospect permission implicitly to infer one—is still a lie. ("He *did* say—didn't he, Mother—that we'd get better returns from him than from our old advisor?" "Why, yes, Father...that is, I *think* he did.")

And that lie sets all your clients up to become disappointed, at some greater or lesser rate of progression, as it becomes increasingly clear to them that you cannot consistently deliver "outperformance." When someone has been with you long enough to determine that, in fact, you can't do what you allowed him to infer that you could do, he leaves—most often, to go to a new liar. So your business, and that of all the other retailers of untruth, is a treadmill to oblivion: you have to keep finding new people to mislead with the chimera of consistent "outperformance," as the old clients progressively reach their threshold of frustration, and slip out the back door.

Again, this is almost incomprehensible, because no one is asking you to say, "I can't deliver consistent outperformance." What this book is asking you to disclose is the simple truth that *no advisor can consistently deliver "outperformance," that the difference is that you're not willing to lie about that fact, and that you offer a much more practical and reliable way to achieve superior long-term, real-life results.*

You're not saying, "I have no clothes." You're the brave lad who was willing to say what everybody else knew but was afraid to say for fear of looking foolish: *"The emperor has no clothes."* (He may have five stars, but he's got no clothes.)

4. THAT A PRACTICE BASED ON THE IMPLICIT UNTRUTH OF CONSISTENTLY DELIVERABLE "OUT-PERFORMANCE" WILL BE ESSENTIALLY REFERRAL-FREE. One of the enduring myths of the financial advisory profession is that clients give you referrals. (This myth is subscribed to even by advisors with 500 clients and zero referrals.) The reality is that advisors get referrals—and even introductions—from *clients who are really happy with them.*

Clients who have been sold the untruth of "outperformance" are never happy. They are almost immediately unhappy, and get progressively unhappier until they leave. Hence, they never refer people to you. Why would they want to set up a friend, relative or esteemed colleague to be disappointed, as they have been?

If you believe, as I do, that every advisor eventually becomes too old, too busy, too tired and/or too bored to prospect any more, then you believe that—without a fairly consistent referral/introduction pipeline—all advisory practices begin to die at exactly that point.

Either (a) you prospect, or (b) happy clients prospect for you, or (c) your practice rolls over and starts tail-spinning toward the deck. (This is yet another reason—if you needed another one—never, ever to have unhappy clients. *Any* unhappy clients, regardless of why they're unhappy. Because they'll never refer you.)

A CAUTIONARY NOTE

Right about now, there is some danger that you have completely accepted that consistent "outperformance" can never be delivered by the retail financial advisor—and have decided that I'm endorsing, or must be about to endorse, passive investing, or indexing.

You're wrong. For reasons that will become clear to you, I'm totally indifferent, in this book, to the issue of active vs. passive investing, as indeed I'm basically indifferent to all issues of portfolio selection. (The one thing I'm not indifferent to with regard to portfolio construction—indeed, the one thing I'm most passionate about—is, as you'll see, asset allocation. But that's a completely different issue.) Moreover, you've missed the point. Because the Kool-Aid of selection is still coursing through your system, you still think active vs. passive, or any selection decision that takes place inside the portfolio, must be critical. It isn't.

The only thing that matters is behavior. You may reality-test this thesis by asking yourself either or both of the following questions:

All successful long-term investing is goal-oriented and therefore planning-driven. All unsuccessful investing is market-oriented and performance-driven. An income you cannot outlive in retirement, a hand in the education of your grandchildren, and significant legacies to the people you love and must leave behind in the world are financial goals; they can and must be planned and invested for. Beating an index, a benchmark, the market or another investor (much less most all other investors) isn't a financial goal, and can't be consistently achieved.

Goal-focused investing is, in that sense, prelapsarian: it's what Adam and Eve did in the Garden of Eden, before the serpent

1. Is an investor in a beautifully diversified portfolio of index funds/ETFs any less likely than an active investor to move his money into nanotechnology funds (or whatever the next bubble is) after two years of 100% annual returns?

2. Is an investor in an S&P 500 index fund any less likely to panic out of it during a 30% market decline (which we get, on average, one year in five) than is an investor in an actively managed big-cap blend fund?

You should, as you read these two questions, begin to feel the fever breaking. That's because, when you truthfully answer "no" to both questions—when you acknowledge that the investor's proclivity to bad behavior, and the behavioral advisor's capacity to stop him, must be the decisive variables—you will accept that, in the largest sense, *active vs. passive doesn't matter.* It's an intellectual/analytical approach to a problem which is emotional/behavioral, and therefore, as we've agreed, it cannot be a critical issue.

Now back to the originally scheduled chapter, already in progress.

got hold of them, and told them they could be—with just a little guidance from him—smart enough to "outperform." *"Outperformance" is the apple. Don't bite into it.*

Oh, by the way: should anything in this chapter—much less everything in this chapter—be taken to mean that a disciplined, goal-focused investor and her wise behavioral advisor can't outperform? *Absolutely not.* The Behavioral Investment Counselor—hereinafter, the BIC—simply refuses to claim (much less promise) "outperformance" before the fact. He neither can nor does rule it out, and he will exert himself within reason—assuming he has chosen the path of active investing—to its achievement.

The BIC simply but passionately makes five categorical statements:

1. "Outperformance," while it may be desirable, can neither be consistently predicted nor controlled by him nor by any other advisor.

2. He does not, therefore—because he cannot, scientifically— assert that his portfolios will "outperform" some other advisor's selections, *and he would very much appreciate being extended the same courtesy by all other advisors.*

3. The issue is fairly academic, anyway, because relative performance is the very smallest component of long-term, real-life return—no more than 10%, and probably less than that.

4. The dominant determinant of long-term, real-life return will be the behavior of the client herself.

5. The BIC's value to his client—the thing that is worth to her multiples of what she must pay him—is as a behavioral coach. The client should be invited to consider that everything else he does for her portfolio—asset allocation, fund/manager/ securities selection, rebalancing, reporting, service, *everything other than behavior modification*—he is cheerfully providing at no charge. *The client must completely buy into the BIC's behavioral value proposition, or they must agree to disagree, and part friends.*

Perhaps, then, just before moving on to an explication of the behavioral value proposition, we ought to amplify the statement we found the BIC formulating at the end of the Introduction, back on page 9:

"I DON'T SAY THAT THE INVESTMENTS I RECOMMEND WILL 'OUTPERFORM' MOST OF YOUR NEIGHBORS' INVESTMENTS.

"I CERTAINLY DON'T RULE IT OUT; I JUST CAN'T PROMISE IT—NOR CAN ANY OTHER ADVISOR—AND IT HAS ALMOST NO CONNECTION WITH WHAT I DO FOR MY CLIENTS.

"I SAY THAT, USING THE PRINCIPLES I PRACTICE, YOU SHOULD END UP WITH A FAR BETTER LIFETIME RETURN THAN DO MOST OF YOUR NEIGHBORS.

"SEEING THAT THESE ARE TWO DIFFERENT THINGS, AND WHY THEY'RE TWO DIFFERENT THINGS, IS THE BEGINNING OF WISDOM—AND THE BEGINNING OF AN UNDERSTANDING OF WHAT I DO."

> Each chapter in this book is followed by a bullet-point summary of its key ideas. The intent is twofold: to let you pause for review before going on, *and to give you, in effect, a mechanism for re-reading the book in its entirety any time you want to.* **You'll find that you can read all the chapter summaries straight through in about 30 minutes.**

1

SUMMARY

§ There is good evidence that over 20-year periods the average equity mutual fund investor will behaviorally do himself out of nearly 60% of the return produced by the average equity mutual fund. He thus underperforms not just the market but his own investments.

§ He does this through a series of fairly common, fairly predictable behavioral mistakes—performance-chasing, speculative euphoria at market tops and panicky capitulation at bottoms, to cite three of the more chronic misbehaviors.

§ The advisor who attempts to resolve this problem through heightened intellectual effort aimed at improving portfolio returns is doomed. The wise advisor will address the central behavioral problem by offering his decisive abilities as a behavioral coach.

§ "Outperformance" is neither a financial goal nor a plan for the attainment of financial goals.

§ There is no statistical evidence for the persistence of performance. This means that attempting to forecast future performance by extrapolating past performance (absolute and/or relative) is the ultimate fool's errand.

⚕ An advisory practice based even implicitly on claims to consistently superior performance, in addition to missing the main behavioral point, is one which must constantly be in the process of disappointing all its clients. It is offering something the advisor can never consistently deliver. Such a practice will also be virtually referral-free.

⚕ The issue of active vs. passive investing is, for the purposes of this book, moot. Since relative portfolio performance is the very smallest determinant of long-term, real-life returns, active vs. passive cannot and does not matter.

⚕ All successful long-term investing is goal-oriented and therefore planning-driven. All unsuccessful investing is market-oriented and performance-driven. Adam and Eve were goal-focused investors…until the serpent got to them. "And we've got to get ourselves back to the garden."

⚕ If only to make the point in its starkest, simplest terms, the BIC should invite the prospect to perceive that all her portfolio services: asset allocation, fund selection, rebalancing, reporting and ordinary service—everything ***other than*** behavior modification—are provided without charge, ***and that her entire fee is in consideration of her value as a behavior modifier***.

⚕ The BIC certainly cannot and does not rule out the possibility that his portfolios will "outperform." He simply refuses to make any forward-looking statement about a variable that can neither be predicted nor controlled, ***and he will appreciate being extended the same courtesy by all other advisors***.

2

THE BEHAVIORAL ADVISOR'S
VALUE PROPOSITION

IF I SAY—OR SIMPLY ALLOW MY PROSPECT TO WALK
away with the impression that I said—that the way I earn my compensation is to perform the selection and timing functions better
than, and thus "outperform," most other advisors, I've painted myself into a corner.

To wit: I must deliver "outperformance" pretty consistently, or have
the investor conclude that I am taking his money but not delivering what he paid me for. As we observed in the previous chapter,
when he reaches the latter conclusion (because I can never deliver
the former benefit), he will leave.

If I make no representations whatsoever about relative "performance"—if I begin with the premise that neither I nor anyone
else can consistently predict or control it—I can virtually never be
taken to task, much less lose an account, on this issue.

But I'd better hurry up and figure out the answer to the question: if I'm not selling "performance," what the heck *am* I selling?

What do I offer that is worth more to the client than what I am proposing to charge him for it? Because that, in its purest essence, is my *value proposition.* It's the answer to the question:

WHAT IS IT THAT I CAN CONSISTENT-LY DO FOR PEOPLE THAT THEY WILL READILY PERCEIVE AS BEING WORTH TO THEM MUCH MORE THAN I'M CHARGING THEM FOR IT?

It should be clear to you that the issue of perception is critical, here. It is nowhere near enough for me actually to be delivering value in excess of what I charge. *The client has to perceive—and appreciate—that I am doing so.* Only when he does perceive this is there any chance that he will be happy with what I'm doing for him. Only when he is happy with what I am doing for him will he refer—or, even better, introduce—me to someone else.

If and to the extent that you ever have an unhappy client—regardless of the infinite variety of ways in which the unhappiness may manifest itself—the cause is always fundamentally the same. **The client comes to believe that what he is getting from you is less valuable than what you are charging him for it.** This can range anywhere from "You're not outperforming" to "I can get the same things you do much cheaper from an online/discount broker" to "You never call me, and when you do, it's only to sell me something" to "I just don't like you anymore."

Don't isolate on the presenting symptoms of the dissatisfaction. Reason always from first principles and look for the universal root cause: *in the client's perception, which is the only thing that matters, your value proposition went negative.*

So the challenge becomes twofold: (1) to develop a service (or a basket of services) that is worth much more to the client than he is asked to pay for it, and (2) to cause the client to perceive, and to persist in the perception, that (1) is true.

It's obviously a lot easier for a planner to do this than for someone who is just an investment advisor. If all I do is manage the client's investments—in a vacuum, away from his essential financial and estate planning—it's going to be that much harder for me to convince him that my value has nothing to do with "performance." This is yet another reason why you don't want to be—and especially don't want yourself to be perceived as being—just a portfolio manager.

But if I'm the planner first—the steward of the household/family's most cherished financial goals—and the portfolio manager second, it's almost inexpressibly easier for the clients to focus on my essential value to them, and how completely it transcends guessing which small-cap value raindrop will get to the bottom of the window before all the other, similar raindrops.

(Note: when a planner starts getting hectored by a client about portfolio "performance," her value proposition has well and truly gone negative, and the account is short term. I assume I need hardly add that she has no one to blame for this but herself, since somewhere along the line she surrendered control of the agenda.)

To apprehend the behavioral value proposition in its simplest and most compelling terms, let's go back to the terrible average large cap fund/average investor dichotomy which we observed in the last chapter, for the 20 years through 2007. Again, these are average annual compound rates of total return, with dividends reinvested:

AVERAGE EQUITY FUND	AVERAGE EQUITY FUND INVESTOR
10.81%	4.48%

We decided that all the average investor in the average large cap fund would have had to do to capture its 10.81% annual net return would have been to leave it alone, and that he was incapable of doing that. He kept moving to different funds; he went into and out of the markets on an alternating current of euphoria and panic; *whatever.* He actively sought, by managing his portfolio rather than himself, to improve its return—and ended up blowing almost 60% of the average return which was effortlessly available to him. This, we concluded, was an anecdotal but quite convincing demonstration of the reality that, in addition to being neither predictable nor controllable in any scientific way,

INVESTMENT PERFORMANCE IS IRRELEVANT.

That is, it has no significant bearing on the long-term, real-life return of real people, *the dominant determinant of which is their own behavior.*

We proceed from this realization to the first of two questions which will define the ability of the Behavioral Investment Counselor to state a simple but inarguable behavioral value proposition:

> IF ALL WE COULD HAVE DONE, OVER THESE 20 YEARS, WAS TO PUT OUR CLIENTS IN THE MOST MUNDANE LARGE CAP EQUITY FUNDS AVAILABLE AND CONVINCE THEM NOT TO MAKE THE GREAT BEHAVIORAL MISTAKES WHICH THEY ACTUALLY MADE...TO WHAT EXTENT WOULD WE HAVE IMPROVED THEIR AVERAGE ANNUAL COMPOUND RETURN?

The purely arithmetic answer for this particular 20 year period is obviously 6.33%—the difference between the 10.81% they would have gotten, in the hypothesis posed by the question above, and the 4.48% they actually (behaviorally) secured for themselves, either on their own or with the tender mercies of a string of selection-and-timing-oriented "advisors."

Take all the time you need to make sure you understand this, not just as an intellectual exercise but as a powerfully liberating emotional/behavioral truth. We are assuming that we had the incredibly rare genius to choose for our clients, from all the hundreds of large cap equity mutual funds available during these 20 years, the single perfect mediocrity. We are attributing the entire shortfall between the fund's return and that earned by the average investor to a series of hard-wired, predictable, consistent, human mistakes. We are, finally, assuming that we prevented the client from making those mistakes, *and that that's all we did for him for 20 years.* Under those assumptions, what would have happened?

Of course: *the gap between investment return and investor return would have closed.* That is, the average investor's return, liberated from his own inappropriate behavioral proclivities, would have ratcheted up from 4.48% to 10.81%, *a pickup in annual return of—shall we say, among friends?—*

SIX HUNDRED BASIS POINTS.

This is the answer to the first of two questions which frame the issue of the behavioral value proposition. Remember that all value propositions are a juxtaposition of what the client gets, and what the provider of that value charges. We have now answered the first question on average for the period under discussion. The client blessed with our unerring behavioral counsel *and nothing else* picks up (or rather would have picked up, over this particular 20 year period) something in the neighborhood of six percent a year.

The second and final question asks:

WHAT DID THE BEHAVIORAL INVESTMENT
COUNSELOR CHARGE THE CLIENT FOR HER
CONSISTENT BEHAVIORAL ADVICE?

The answer to this question will be assumed to work out to something in the neighborhood of one percent per year, or

ONE HUNDRED BASIS POINTS.

Two observations about this second number are in order.

First, I neither know, care nor have any recommendation about how you get to this number. For purposes of this very basic discussion of the behavioral value proposition, take it as the "plug" number that it is. Whether you are fee-based, fee-only, commissioned, on retainer or involved in bartering your advice for food, clothing and dental care is a matter of complete indifference—nay, of stupefying boredom—to me at this point. It does not and indeed cannot matter: *I'm assuming you charge about a point.*

(That said, I do hope and expect that you are charging separately for the financial plan. My experience is that if you give people a plan for free they won't follow it, reasoning that it's probably worth about what they had to pay for it. Moreover, if you throw in the plan for free while charging ostensibly only for the portfolio management, people will just naturally assume that the latter is far more important than the former—a fatal mistake.)

The second caveat is that the hundred basis points to which I refer are assumed to be your and your firm's charges purely for advice—*over and above the management costs built into the investments themselves, which an investor would have to pay anyway, even if—heaven forbid—he didn't have you.*

This, then, in its simplest form, is a calibration of the BIC's value proposition. That value proposition should be intuitive: *you will do far better, in real life, with an empathetic, tough-loving behavioral coach than you will on your own, or with some bozo who keeps babbling about standard deviation when you're having a panic attack in a bear market.* Sadly, this epiphany is anything but intuitive. So one is reduced to this graphic if somewhat ham-handed explanation:

> OVER THESE 20 YEARS, THE AVERAGE
> INVESTOR IN THE AVERAGE LARGE
> CAP FUND WOULD HAVE PAID ABOUT
> ONE HUNDRED BASIS POINTS FOR
> ADVICE THAT WOULD HAVE IMPROVED
> HIS RETURN BY SOMETHING LIKE SIX
> HUNDRED BASIS POINTS.

Having made this point as pithily as we can, we must obviously now rush to qualify it. We want people to know what it says, but we'd better be equally sure that they know what it does *not* say.

1. First and foremost, it does not say anything that sounds even a little bit like, "Pay me one to make six." That's not an anecdotal/hypothetical example: it's a forward-looking statement that has gone over to the dark side. It's a projection. And if there's anything I've learned for absolute certain in 40 years in this business, it's that *he who lives by projections dies—slowly, and in great pain—by projections.*

2. Nor is it safe even to suggest that the incremental gains from behavior management will outweigh their cost by anything like the margin they would have over these 20 years. That may sound like the same point I just made, but it's different. This aspect of the above no-no is that *it suggests, however implicitly, that the prospect is the average investor—a notion that he can be expected violently to reject...especially if it's true.*

Like the 80% of all drivers who rate themselves above average—or the citizens of Garrison Keillor's Lake Wobegon, where all the children are above average—nobody believes himself to be the average investor. Thus, any permutation of the "pay me one to make six" conclusion is going to snap back in your face, so hard it will make your head spin.

Again: *all we're attempting here is an illustration.* We're trying to show the tremendous extent to which inappropriate behavior is destructive of long-term returns, and therefore—just logically—how valuable a behavioral advisor might be, absolutely *and* relative to his cost.

> "TRY TO THINK OF MY ONE PERCENT COST AS THE ANNUAL PREMIUM ON A SORT OF 'BIG MISTAKE' INSURANCE POLICY. EXCEPT THAT, UNLIKE OTHER INSURANCES, THE POLICY THAT I PRO-VIDE PAYS OFF BEFORE A DISASTER HAPPENS. THAT'S BECAUSE, RATHER THAN REPAIRING THE DAMAGE, I'VE WORKED WITH YOU TO PREVENT IT."

3. And we can't—and must not appear to—guarantee that, even if he pays the premium on his policy, the client won't still figure out a way to steer around us, and drive over a cliff.

The BIC can empathize, reason and encourage a client not to panic out of a lifetime equity portfolio when it's down 30% in a bear market. *But he can't actually stop the poor wretch.* He can actively, convincingly and even passionately dissuade a client from putting two thirds of his portfolio into nanotechnology (again, my proxy for the next "new era") after it's gone up 100% a year for two years. But the client can—and some will—still run over him (crying the four-word death song of the American investor: *"This time is different").*

In the end, behavioral investment counseling—like diet, exercise, and taking prescribed medication—only works if the patient does what the doctor advises. Doctor Noah, the Behavioral Investment Counselor, cannot (in this analogy, which is a very important one) flatten one's abs, clean out one's arteries or force-feed a patient his meds. This truth brings us face to face with the first great law of Behavioral Investment Counseling, which you will see repeated over and over throughout this book:

YOU CAN ONLY HELP PEOPLE WHO ARE WILLING TO BE HELPED, NOW, BY YOU.

You cannot help someone who is refusing to be helped—in other words, to take your advice. Advisors constantly ask me questions that start with, "How do you convince people that…?" I don't usually wait to hear how the sentence ends, because I don't need to. My answer is always the same: I don't know how to convince anybody of anything. Moreover, I think trying to convince people is beneath my dignity…and yours.

A doctor doesn't convince; he prescribes. It's a totally different function. He can, and quite often does, say things like, "You need to get less red meat and more vegetables and fruit in your diet, and to start a regular exercise program, and to take this prescription blood thinner, because I find you to be at very high risk of a stroke or a heart attack, either of which could disable or kill you." *He cannot then force someone not to die.* I believe it's just as simple as that.

4. Finally, you don't even want to suggest that 4.48% and 10.81% are in any sense absolute numbers. They will, as I suggested earlier, bounce around all over the place. What we BICs intuitively believe in is the *relationship* between the two numbers, whatever those numbers happen to be at the end of any other 20 year period. *We believe, in other words, that the average investor figures out a series of behavioral ways to fritter away far more than half of the return of the average fund over any two decades—that he underperforms not just the market but his own investments.* We think this general relationship is well-nigh immutable, because we know that it's caused by human nature, which we're absolutely *sure* is immutable.

And in that thought, oddly enough, is a perception which frees us from any particular 20-year set of numbers, and which has the potential to be even more powerful. It is the idea—which we must convey with great circumspection—that sound behavioral advice, faithfully followed, might have much more than *doubled* the average return of the average fund investor, *simply by weeding out the toxic, hard-wired emotional behaviors which have historically cost him upwards of 60% of the average available return.*

It takes a special kind of advisor to apprehend the decisive importance of behavior in the real lives of real people. It takes an even more special and courageous advisor to espouse behavior modification as both a mission and a value proposition. Finally, it takes a pretty special kind of client to actually heed the behavioral message—to say, "Sure, I'd like to own nothing but top-performing investments all the time, but mostly I'd like someone to help me stay on the straight and narrow, and to keep me from shooting myself in the foot."

But make no mistake about it: the epiphany on the prospect's part— "Hey, it's not so much what my funds do; it's what I do; and I can be really well-coached in that regard by somebody I trust and like"—is a response to something. In this society, people are not going to wander into your office and spontaneously ask for behavioral guidance. They're going to ask for the wrong thing; the BIC is going to offer them an understanding of the right thing; and then they're either going to get it or they're not. For many are called, but few are chosen.

The question for the potential BIC is simply: what, if anything, will induce the prospective client to have the epiphany he needs to have? What provokes the response we are looking for: the realization that behavior is his essential problem, and that a behavioral coach is not just *an* answer but *the* answer?

Clearly, there's no chart, graph or scattergram that will prove to someone that he needs behavioral coaching, and that relative "performance"—in addition to being unpredictable and uncontrollable with any precision—is actually irrelevant to long-term, real-life returns. So what will make your prospect see the light?

The answer, of course, is that you will—or nothing will. I can help a little—maybe even more than a little—with my book for clients,

Simple Wealth, Inevitable Wealth, in which I make the case, in layman's terms, that long-term investment success is improbable in the extreme without the help of a gifted behavioral advisor. You can use that book to very good effect, but—and here's the essential point—you can't hide behind it. You can't *make* this "sale:" you have to *be* the "sale." The essence of what needs to happen here can be summed up perfectly in this gnomic sentence:

THE MESSENGER IS THE MESSAGE.

You are the epiphany—or there is no epiphany. This implies a professional life of glorious freedom—from the economy, from the markets, from the randomness of relative "performance"—but it also imposes an equal burden of personal responsibility on you. Your behavioral advice can become the critical input in your clients' investing careers; that's inarguable at this point.

But no one will ever believe that about you, unless and until you believe it about yourself. Advisors seem not to see that it is their own belief that induces their prospects to believe, and their own self-doubt that induces skepticism: over a large sample of prospect/client interviews, we get back pretty much what we put forth.

But the basic argument has already been made. You ought to be very sure you understand that argument intellectually, and that you are very powerfully drawn to it emotionally. If you still have many questions, all well and good; I'll do my best to answer them as we go along. But right here, right now, you'd better ask yourself a question. And it isn't "Can I sell this?" It's

DO I BELIEVE THIS?

2

SUMMARY

  A value proposition is a statement by the purveyor of a service to the effect that its value is much greater to the consumer of that service than the consumer is asked to pay for it. For the value proposition to be accepted, the consumer must agree that the service is worth much more to him than it costs, *and he must persist in this belief.* If and when the consumer comes to believe that the cost is greater than the value of the service, he will end the relationship.

  It is immeasurably easier for a planner, who manages portfolios only as a funding medium for the plan, to establish his value than it is for someone who is merely a portfolio manager to do so.

  The behavioral value proposition is virtually self-evident: *if behavior has historically cost the average investor anything like six hundred basis points per year, and if behavior management costs only about one hundred basis points per year, the point is made.* It remains only for the investor to (a) accept his own inappropriate behavior as the key retardant of his return to date, and (b) accept the BIC's advice, and resolve to follow it.

  This last point is critical. If a physical trainer prescribes a program of diet and exercise, and the client doesn't work the program, he won't lose weight or improve his fitness. It isn't enough for the BIC to render great advice; *the client has to follow it.* Accept that you have very limited control over that. Accept that you can only help people who are willing to be helped, now, by you.

§ The messenger is the message. You have to become one with your behavioral advice. No one will ever believe you unless your own belief in the primacy of behavioral advice is the essential aspect of your professional identity.

§ The question, therefore, isn't "Can I sell this?" It's

"DO I BELIEVE THIS?"

3

THE VALUE OF TIME

SUPPOSE YOU ARE GOING ALONG, RUNNING AN ES-
tablished business, and looking to make a significant jump in assets
under management and income. Suppose further that you have
room to triple the time and energy you put into one—**but only
one**—professional pursuit. I think it just stands to reason that you
will choose to triple your time/energy investment in the one pursuit which can yield you the greatest incremental assets to manage,
along with the additional income thereon.

Suppose you chose to triple your input into prospecting, referral/in-
troduction-seeking, and getting relentlessly deeper into your existing clients' financial lives. Question: do you believe that, over time,
this would lead inevitably to a tripling of your AUM and income?

Well, of course it would. How could it not? These pursuits are heav-
en's own original numbers game, and if you triple the inputs—**and
don't stop**—the outcomes must surely triple in the fullness of time.
(If you viscerally disbelieve this hypothesis, you are at least situation-
ally depressed, and I fear there is some chance that you are clinically
depressed. A startling percentage of stressed-out advisors, running on

the treadmill to oblivion that is a selection-and-timing, "perfor-mance"-driven practice, are in fact quite seriously depressed.)

Now suppose that, instead of investing your capacity for tripling your input into client acquisition/development, you decided to put it into deeper study of financial and estate planning. Would this lead, directly or even indirectly, to a tripling of your effectiveness as a financial planner—forgetting, for the moment, its effect on AUM and income?

Here I think we must conclude that we're just not sure. We would certainly be learning a great deal more—if volume of knowledge is the appropriate measure—but would we be continuing to learn more things of paramount, and even critical, importance? Or would we, as our study became progressively subtler and more nu-anced, simply be refining the big ideas we already knew? In other words, would the marginal utility of all the new knowledge—its importance and usefulness *compared to what we already know*—make us thrice as effective as advisors?

I rather think not. I suspect that the law of diminishing returns will set in long before we've studied for that last incremental hour, or expended that last incremental erg of energy, such that the relative importance of each new thing we're learning will be in significant decline. And I don't see how that can lead to a major improvement in our business.

Finally, suppose you chose to invest your tripled capacity in study-ing the economy, the behavior of the capital markets, and the fac-tors which can produce superior relative "performance." *Would it be reasonable to assume that your clients' portfolio returns would then triple?*

You scoff at this question—and well you might. You intuitively real-ize from bitter experience that even if you were to triple your study of these variables, the incremental return to your clients' portfolios would at best be much, much less than three times. Moreover, you probably suspect that there might not in practice be any incremental improvement at all—and that there is at least some chance that the net return could actually be *negative*, since **it so often seems that the more you study these variables, the more wrong you become.**

And yet tomorrow, instead of having meetings with the three clients who seemed most spooked by the market's last 10% decline—i.e. clients who give evidence of being susceptible to one of investing's greatest behavioral mistakes, namely panic selling—you're planning to go to another fund manager's due diligence meeting.

There you will hear an economist give an economic forecast that will either turn out to be right or wrong, followed by the fund's chief investment strategist, who will spin a market viewpoint that just happens to favor his fund or funds. Your ability to forecast the economy or the markets will not have improved one iota when this meeting is over—nor will your ability to control your clients' proclivities to inappropriate behavior.

What we're conducting here is a serious inquiry into **the value of your time** as an organizing principle in a retail financial advisory practice, with special attention paid to the law of diminishing returns.

All advisors—indeed, all businesspeople—are constantly making very finely calibrated judgments about the value of their time all day long, without ever necessarily being conscious that they're do-ing so. How? By choosing to do the next thing that they've chosen to do—which is also a decision **not** to do all the other things they might have chosen to do at that precise moment in time, and with that quantum of energy.

In the year 2007, if you can believe this, I actually received two separate, unrelated e-mails from advisors, claiming that they had each been charged $2.50 too much for shipping and handling on books that they had ordered from me. Each stated his rationale for this conclusion, and requested a $2.50 refund. In the interest of full disclosure, perhaps I should amend the foregoing statement:

each of these blighted souls had his assistant send me the e-mail, presumably because he was so ashamed.

Observe the fact pattern: advisor takes time to check the shipping and handling charge on his receipt, then takes time to compare this to what he thinks it should have been, and concludes that it's over by $2.50. (Each is wrong on the facts, but that is totally irrelevant to the point I'm making.) He then takes time to explain his erroneous reasoning to his assistant, who takes time to understand said reasoning. She then takes time to write and send the e-mail, providing a copy to the advisor which he then takes time to read.

Even if advisor and assistant are both lightning fast at this, I don't think there's any way they can have accomplished all this in much less than five man-minutes (that is, counting one minute when they were talking to each other as two man-minutes). Now remember: their total upside—the maximum potential return on these five man-minutes—is $2.50.

It should be clear to you that advisor and assistant have set a blended value on their time of 50 cents a minute, or $30 an hour. Let's assume that's split $10 to her and $20 to him, just because I can't guess what else to assume. That means he's probably earning about what a letter carrier for the U.S. Postal Service makes, with benefits.

The advisor has now said: the highest and best use of the next five man-minutes his practice has is not to call a prospect, not to write a birthday card to a client, not to bone up on the new IRA distribution rules, not to read the Fed chairman's most recent Congressional testimony, *but to try to recover $2.50 from me which I do not even owe him.* Just because he didn't say this out loud—nor even formulate it consciously in his mind—actions speak louder than words, and *that's what he said, for all the universe to hear.*

If you focus on the grotesqueness of the fact pattern—the dollars involved—you'll have missed the point of this story, which is of course about the concept of setting a price on your time, and then making absolutely sure that you're always delivering real, *perceptible* value far in excess of that wage.

Let's assume that you want to be worth to your clients, and therefore to earn—for that has to be the sequence—$500,000 per year. Let's say further that your practice nets you, before taxes, 50% of its gross revenues. (This could be because you're a million-dollar producer on 50% payout in a wirehouse, or because you're an independent practitioner whose rent, staff salaries and other expenses sum to $500,000. Or whatever.)

I believe that you can work at most about 1800 hours a year. Your gross potential days worked are five days a week for 52 weeks; that's 260 days. I hope you're taking a good three weeks of vacation, and there are upwards of 10 civil or religious holidays you won't work. You're going out of town for one wedding, one funeral and one graduation, you're sure to qualify for at least one of your firm's award trips, and you're going to be sick a couple of days.

Plus, don't you just need a mental health day now and again? Give me the umpty-umpth rainy, cold March day on Long Island when nobody else is home, and I'm gonna unplug the phone and watch the Beatles Anthology all the way through. (And be a better man for having done so.) At eight solid hours on each and every one of the remaining days, 1800 hours is just the flat-out most I can ever see you being able to put in.

And every time I divide those 1800 hours you've got for sale into the million dollars we've just agreed your practice has to gross in a year, I get five hundred and fifty-five American dollars. Why don't we just call it an even $500 an hour?

Now, you may be saying, "Well, I'm not asking any one client to pay me $500 an hour, the way a top estate attorney or litigator does. I'm asking my whole practice to pay me $500 an hour, which isn't the same thing." I wouldn't argue with this narrow construction. I'd simply point out that (a) you're asking *some-*

body to pay you $500 an hour, and (b) you'd better have a very clear and focused idea of what you do that might be worth $500 an hour *to anybody or everybody.*

Thus, our first principle must be that a senior advisor should be performing only those tasks which are of critical importance to the long-term financial success of the client household/family. These are, I believe, the only tasks which could be fairly valued at $500 an hour. There are very few such critical tasks, and we'll enumerate them in just a few moments.

The second principle of organization of effort is that the senior advisor should be aiming to deliver solutions to the highest needs of the client with the least expenditure of time and effort. As Voltaire famously observed, the best is the enemy of the good. That is, a neurotic striving for perfection in each and every case will effectively prevent an advisor from having a large practice full of clients he can serve quite well.

And the third principle—strongly implied by the second—is that the senior advisor should stop any activity at the point of diminishing returns. When each additional hour of his time yields not greater but smaller value to the clients and the practice, the advisor should either hand it off to a subordinate *or stop it altogether.*

For example, suppose you find that you can move your clients' portfolio returns from the riskless 5.3% historically offered by the long-term Treasury bond to a blended 11.5%, assuming half the portfolio is in large-cap common stocks and the other half in small-cap, consistent with the long-term returns of both indexes. And suppose you discover that you can do this with the expenditure of 100 of your budgeted 1800 hours per year.

Next, suppose you came to believe that, with the input of another 100 hours—in other words, a doubling of your work on timing and selection—you could probably move that return to 13% (accepting, of course, some possibility that after the second hundred hours the return might not have gone up that much, if at all).

Clearly, no rational businessperson would attempt this. Doubling one's time and effort in the by-no-means assured quest for a relatively minor increment in total return is simply begging to get crushed by the operation of the iron law of diminishing returns. ***This is even more terribly true if a client was, all along, perfectly capable of achieving all his most cherished financial goals with anything even approaching 11.5% a year.***

And that, finally, is the point of these three organizational principles. The BIC is not attempting to get her clients the maximum possible returns (whatever that means). She is trying to get competitive returns which will fulfill her clients' financial goals with the minimum expenditure of time, energy and stress.

What, then, are the critically valuable tasks which the senior advisor should be directly involved in—other than client acquisition and development—and in what order of importance? Keeping our eyes on the ($500 an hour) prize, I believe we'd conclude that they are:

1. FORMAL FINANCIAL AND ESTATE PLANNING, AND THE STRATEGIC MAINTENANCE OF SAID PLANS. This is the highest, best and most valuable use of a financial advisor's time and energy. The plan drives everything else; on any day when it does not, both the client and the advisor have lost their way. Note, too, that the phrase I use for upkeep of the plan is *strategic maintenance*, as opposed to getting some form signed and filed. Once a plan is in place, the senior advisor should touch it only for the formal annual review, and when a major life change and/or goal change occurs.

2. GOAL-FOCUSED INVESTMENT PLANNING. The only rational long-term investment policy is one designed to meet the lifetime and multigenerational financial goals of the household/family. If we assume, therefore, that the protection needs, i.e. insurance against what can go wrong, have been served above, in the financial planning phase, we now have the luxury of investing for what can go right: the endowment of a retirement income the clients don't outlive, the best educations for which their children and grandchildren qualify, and significant legacies to the people they love and must leave behind in the world. Note well that goal-focused investment planning *is entirely unaffected by market events.*

3. BEHAVIOR MANAGEMENT AND MODIFICATION.

This is the critical, ongoing function of helping clients not to blow up their own beautifully crafted financial plans and (much more to the point of this book) their own rationally asset-allocated and elegantly diversified portfolios of the right **kinds** of investments necessary to the realization of their most important financial goals.

4. INVESTMENT SELECTION.

I exclude timing altogether as a valuable pursuit, because of what I regard as its inherent impossibility. I concede that selection—in actively managed portfolios—may be an intelligent use of **some** time and effort **subordinate to the three pursuits listed above.** (I'll offer some highly personal guidelines for manager selection in a later chapter, if you're still interested.) In sum, selection may be largely irrelevant, but timing is simply unthinkable.

You will find it extremely useful, as you plan a day's (or even a week's) work, to enter each task you propose to perform under one of these four headings—again excepting only client acquisition/development, which is not, strictly speaking, a service performed for your clients. (I certainly do not intend to slight it for that reason; indeed, I regard a day in which no such activity takes place as wasted, and even dangerous. A practice which is not growing is dying, and few if any practices grow to their full potential without some systematic daily nurturing by the senior advisor.)

When you can see, in writing, where you're putting your time and energy relative to this hierarchy of where they will yield the most value, you'll have a very good idea of why your practice is performing as it is.

If you do not consciously put your effort to its best use, I can pretty much guarantee that it will get siphoned off into less—and maybe much less—valuable pursuits. I was waiting to catch a flight not long ago with an advisor who had just come from the meeting at which I'd spoken.

He was a CPA who had started an investment advisory practice in the full expectation that it would be purely additive to his accounting practice, and had found—as many such people do—that the two practices were actually at war with each other, with him in the crossfire. His income, far from being added to, was being diluted by this conflict. "I keep getting pulled into things I don't want to get pulled into," he complained.

I told him, as politely as I could, that an adult human being—and particularly one who is his own boss—can never actually have the experience of being forced to do something he doesn't want to do. If he gets pulled into secondary and tertiary pursuits, it's because he didn't want *not* to be pulled into them—at least, not enough to prevent this from happening.

He had ceased to run his business. It was running him...into the ground. Of course his income had stagnated. And of course he was experiencing a lot of stress. He had lost the discipline of maintaining his priorities, and had arrived at the point where he had no priorities. He was no longer acting; he was in a constant state of reaction.

This could not happen to anyone who organized his priorities according to the four categories above, in that order. But regardless of what your priorities are, investment selection has to be at the bottom of them, and timing has to be off the page entirely.

Of course, the simplest and most effective discipline for doing only those activities which are most valuable to the clients—and thus, in the long run, most remunerative to the practice—is simply to refuse to do anything else. The way you do that, in turn, is with paraprofessional and support staff.

If you seriously value your time at $500 an hour, and if you genuinely believe your higher functions are worth such a sum, then you must realize that anything and everything in your practice which **can** be done by someone earning $30 an hour **must** be done by such a person.

Where did I get that number? I was waiting to cross the street, and the number 30 bus went by. What the hell difference does it make? Maybe in your town the number is $25, or even $20. In Manhattan or Beverly Hills, maybe it's $50. Surely you see that the absolute number is irrelevant; it has meaning only in relation to the value of *your* time.

Without excessively personalizing this, I work one heck of a lot less than 1800 hours a year, and earn one heck of a lot more than $500 for each of those hours. There is nothing—absolutely nothing—of a support nature that I can't get done for $50 an hour or less. (The only exceptions to this rule are my attorney and my accountant, both of whom I pay top dollar with a beatific smile on my face, as each has either saved me or made me millions of dollars—far in excess of what I've paid them, *for such is their value proposition*—since we got together about 15 years ago.)

I can compose and edit my books and newsletter on my laptop, wherever I am in the world. (A minority partner publishes the newsletter and does subscription fulfillment, leaving me free to write and edit it, which are my highest-value contributions to it.) My son manages the distribution of my books, and my younger daughter is my bookkeeper, both part-time.

I do my own scheduling with respect to speaking engagements, and I make my own travel arrangements through American Express Centurion Travel. The only thing I do of an even vaguely administrative nature is my expense reports after speaking, because nobody but me can make any sense of them, and I can bang them out in about the time it takes to explain them. **Somebody else does everything else.**

Without in any way minimizing the difficulty of getting and keeping good help—and certainly without getting into the nuances of organizing and managing a staff, about which I know functionally next to nothing—I say: go thou, and do likewise. Anything you need done that can be done by someone who makes a fraction of what you're attempting to make *must be done by that person.* This is the essential discipline that liberates you to focus all your energy and creativity on the activities that matter most.

Keep your eyes on the prize.

3

SUMMARY

$ The value of your time is the key organizing principle in a retail financial advisory practice. You will never earn more than the value you yourself have placed on your professional hour.

$ You are always making exquisitely calibrated judgments about the value of your time, regardless of the fact that those judgments may be entirely unconscious. If you are, at any given moment, doing anything that could be done competently by someone who earns less than you wish to, you have devalued yourself to exactly that extent, and this will show up almost immediately in your earnings.

$ It is doubtful that you can lead any kind of genuinely healthy and balanced life working more than 1800 hours a year. Your earnings will therefore most probably be the value which you set and maintain (consciously or unconsciously) on each of those hours, multiplied by 1800.

$ It will be critical, once you have set a value on your time, to decide which are and which are not high-value uses of that time. Remember that, in each of those hours, you must be rendering service which is *and is perceived by your clients to be* greater than what you are charging for it.

$ Most retail financial advisors have the potential to be somewhere between good and excellent at creating and fostering healthy, productive client relationships. This is a very high-value use of time, because the quality of the relationship is the key to whether a client will accept your behavioral advice. Relationship-building is therefore a pursuit to which you would ideally devote more rather than less time.

§ Most retail financial advisors are also—with the proper technical staff and vendor support—good to excellent financial planners, and are very proficient at allocating assets in the service of a sound long-term plan. *Their focus should be on getting the returns the client needs—not the highest returns in the known universe—with a minimum of time, effort and stress.* These, too, are enterprises into which one would ideally prefer to put more rather than less time.

§ Most retail financial advisors are at best intermittently adequate practitioners of selection and timing. Even more to the point, the incremental yield on increased time invested in this pursuit is subject to a very steep curve of diminishing returns—a curve which can and too often does go negative.

§ Thus, given a finite number of hours, the wise advisor will actually take time away from selection and timing in order to invest it in the more productive pursuits, *and may very well decide to outsource portfolio management altogether.*

§ To the extent that you are not running your business—rigorously allocating your time and energy only to the highest-value pursuits—it will most certainly run you…into the ground.

§ If you ever hope to deserve and earn an excellent income (for that is the sequence, in this business), you must never do anything that you can get done for less than about fifty dollars an hour.

§ Discipline yourself constantly to ask, until you don't need to ask anymore, *"What is the true value to my clients of what I'm doing right this minute?"*

BOOK TWO

THE
BEHAVIORAL
APPROACH
TO SUPERIOR
LIFETIME
RETURNS

4

SIX STEPS TO THE UPPER REACHES

PART 1

IN THE PROCESS OF DETERMINING THE PROFES-
sional functions of the Behavioral Investment Counselor, we have
so far learned two critically important things.

First, he is not primarily trying to identify investments which will
"outperform" most other people's investments; rather, he is trying to
help his clients behave in such a way that they achieve higher long-
term, real-life rates of return than do most other people. The BIC
believes—and never ceases to advocate for his belief—that the value
to the client of this function is a multiple of what he charges for it.

Second, the BIC is not trying to produce the highest possible investment returns—a concept not only neurotic but chimerical, in that
somebody, somewhere is always getting a higher return, if only for
the moment, by taking on much more uncompensated risk. Rather,
he is trying to earn his clients the returns they will need to fund their
most important lifetime (and transgenerational) financial goals with
the minimum expenditure of time, energy and stress. He therefore
creates and maintains portfolios which are fundamentally goal-

driven, as opposed to being driven by any particular economic or market viewpoint, which he regards as irrelevant.

The question now becomes: what exactly is the portfolio management philosophy of a Behavioral Investment Counselor? What does she do—and what does she try to get her clients to do *and not do*—that leads her to espouse the belief that her clients will indeed achieve superior long-term, real-life returns which (a) result in the achievement of the client's most cherished goals and (b) exceed the actual returns earned by the great preponderance of other investors?

Conceptually, the answer is: the BIC concentrates her time and energy on attempting to control variables which (1) can be controlled (as opposed to the short- to intermediate-term peregrinations of the economy and the markets, which cannot), and (2) have the most pronounced effect on long-term, real-life return.

For example, asset allocation—whether and to what extent to be in equities vs. bonds during a three-decade retirement—is orders of magnitude more important than fund/manager selection in determining whether or not retirees will be able to sustain their lifestyle. Many people will run out of money in retirement because they allocated assets unwisely—they took too many fixed-income investments into 30 years of a rising-cost retirement. But virtually no one will run out of money in retirement because of which small-cap value manager he hired, in preference to other small-cap value managers.

This being the case, the BIC will consider asset allocation an almost immeasurably more important variable than selection, and will apportion her time and energy accordingly. Other advisors and their clients will do just the opposite—they will put the great part of their time and energy into trying to figure out which managers will "outperform," with the result that they'll end up chasing their tails *and missing the great strategic truth of asset allocation.*

What, then, are the genuinely critical variables—the most highly controllable beliefs and behaviors which will most reliably, and with the least effort, deliver the BIC's faithful clients to the upper reaches of long-term, real-life return?

After more than 40 years in the financial advisory profession—dealing first directly and now indirectly **but constantly** with the investing public all that time—I'm convinced that there are six variables which dictate 90% of a household/family's lifetime investment return. Three of these are **principles**; that is, they are basic attitudinal approaches to goal-focused long-term investing which take place in the mind of the investor rather than inside the portfolio. The other three steps are **practices**, or methods of managing the portfolio itself.

These are not, as you'll quickly see, six variables of equal weight. The attitudinal/behavioral principles are very much more important to investor outcomes than are the practices. *Indeed, the principles dictate the practices, in the sense that belief always dictates behavior.*

For example, if I believe that the American economy is so fragile and vulnerable that it might at any moment be thrown into a deep, prolonged contraction, I will be predisposed to panicking out of equities even in a mild recession and/or a moderate decline in the equity market. That is, my alarmist belief system will dictate an inappropriate behavioral overreaction, from which my long-term financial plan may never recover.

If, on the other hand, I have great faith—based solidly on the historical record—in the depth, flexibility and resiliency of the economy, and in the ability of monetary policymakers to meliorate any significant weakening, I will probably not panic, but will hold on, and thus participate in the inevitable recovery. My belief system, rather than any intellectual understanding of the economic situation, will dictate the appropriate behavior. Not surprisingly, then, faith in the future will turn out to be the first of the three critical principles.

Just before enumerating and explaining those three principles and three practices, let me spend a moment on the issue of just how important I believe them to be. I said just a moment ago that these six variables will account for upwards of 90% of a client's long-term, real-life investment return. This implies that selection and timing might— I say again, **might**—account for the remaining 10% of return.

If you're prepared to accept the idea that these six variables will govern 90% of real-life return—that they will indeed cause your clients to gain superior outcomes relative to the great preponderance of their neighbors—is there any way to calibrate that margin? *What percentage of people, in other words, will your clients (in the truest sense) "outperform"?*

I wish I knew, and could tell you. Maybe someday the science of behavioral finance will have advanced to the point where such things are objectively quantifiable. But for now, I'm just going to ask you to hold this question in abeyance, simply keeping it in mind as we work through the six steps. At each step, just ask yourself: how much must this be worth to the people who believe and practice it, compared to the returns of people who don't?

The first and greatest of the principles is, of course:

1. FAITH IN THE FUTURE. Candidly, I would love to call this one simply "Faith," without amplification or modifier; I forebear to do so for fear that you would think I were preaching some spiritual principle, rather than a hard-headed economic/historical perspective.

In the long run, I believe that successful investing is essentially a battle that takes place in the investor's unconscious mind—a battle between faith in the future and fear of the future. And in the end—after, say, 40 years of accumulating assets during a working career, followed by another 30 years of living off those assets in retirement—the investor's lifetime return will be to a very great extent governed by which of these impulses wins.

I am certainly not talking about—much less advocating—blind faith, nor mindless optimism that runs contrary to reality. Quite the opposite, and this is the critical point. Faith in the future from an investor's perspective is simply the only worldview which squares with the historical record. We who are endowed with long-term optimism espouse it not in spite of the facts but because of them. In short, *we regard optimism as the only realism.*

It is impossible to live in the world for any length of time without, however reluctantly, concluding that the curve of human progress is not merely rising sharply, but that it's actually accelerating—the curve is bending upwards. Indeed, the huge preponderance of all the medical, scientific, technological and economic progress which mankind has ever experienced has gone on in my lifetime.

My father was born in 1909; his life expectancy was 47 years. I was born in 1943; my life expectancy at birth was 64—an age I've already passed. My grandson Will Dickerson, who shares the dedication of this book, was born in 2002; his life expectancy at birth was 78. (And heaven knows how much his life expectancy will be extended by medical advances during his lifetime, just as yours and mine have been.) That four-generation jump in life expectancy—about 30 years—is roughly equal to the increase which took place between the age of the Neanderthals, 35,000 years ago, and the birth of my father.

In 1918, when he was nine years old, my father's older sister—along with half a million other Americans, and some 22 million people worldwide—died of influenza. My wife Joan, who was born in 1944, had two maternal aunts and two maternal uncles. Before she was six years old, one aunt and one uncle had died of tuberculosis. When I was in the third grade, a girl in my class died of a particularly virulent strain of polio, which suddenly paralyzed her lungs.

These afflictions, and many other common killers and cripplers in living memory, have been all but eradicated in my lifetime—or their incidence is such a non-event that we can joke about it ("Every year that I get a flu shot, I get the flu"). During that period, we have learned 95% of everything we've ever known about the operation of the brain, and flat-out everything we know about DNA and the human genome. We are doing surgery to repair the hearts of fetuses—in some cases, fetuses whose very conception is due to *in vitro* fertilization and other reproductive techniques which were undreamed of when I was born.

Technologically, the world has progressed more just in the last 40 years than it had in all previous human history. That's because the most important invention in the history of mankind—the microprocessor, an entire computer on a tiny chip—took place in 1971. And it has been doubling in capacity (and halving in price) about every two years since. Here, progress clearly isn't linear, it's exponential: in 2006, Intel demonstrated a prototype chip that has 80 specialized computing cores, and roughly the power of a 1996 supercomputer that occupied more than 85 refrigerator-sized cabinets.

My daughter Karen's soccer-mom minivan has anti-lock brakes, a GPS system, a DVD player—and it warns her if she's backing up too close to another object. It offers these features because the microprocessors in today's minivan *contain more computing power than existed on the earth in 1950—and much more than was available to NASA for the entirety of the Apollo 13 mission*. (Buy—do not rent—Ron Howard's magisterial film *Apollo 13*—and watch the world's foremost rocket scientists trying to get those three astronauts home in April 1970 *using slide rules*.)

Funnily enough, this illustrates a reason for investors' occasional inability to stay emotionally tuned in to the breakthroughs surging forward all around them. It's an odd psychological mechanism (in the jargon, a *heuristic*) which I've just this instant decided to call *the commoditization of miracles*. The fact is that all great technological leaps follow the same trajectory from miracle to commodity. From canals to railroads to automobiles to airplanes to radio to TV to xerography to faxes to PCs to cell phones to the Internet itself, every "new era" technology becomes a commonplace, and we quickly learn to take it for granted.

I was riding shotgun in the aforementioned minivan not very long ago; Karen was driving, and my grandchildren Rebecca and Will were in back. We were traveling from Brooklyn Heights to the North Fork (that is, from one end of Long Island to the other), a nice, leisurely hour-and-three-quarter trip.

So Karen put in a DVD of *Finding Nemo*, one of the kids' favorites. I couldn't see it, of course, but I listened to the dialogue, which struck me as both good writing and good acting. I commented on this at the end of the ride, whereupon Rebecca (then six years old) asked me, "What kind of DVDs did you watch in the car when you were little, 'Pa?"

I told her the plain fact: that not only did we not have DVDs in the car when I was six (in 1949): *we didn't have television.* Rebecca blinked a couple of times, trying to find a way to apprehend the enormity of what I'd told her—and then changed the subject.

It will one day be at least as difficult to explain to Will—who at six is a demon Googler—that well within his mother's lifetime you couldn't just go online and effortlessly search for anything and everything that's known in the world. (By the time he's in high school, he will not type his search requests into his PC, but speak them, and the computer will speak back to him—in English, regardless that the answer is on the Web in a different language. The search engine, whether it's Google or some other commodity provider, will have translated it for him.)

What portion of the national treasury would Thomas Jefferson have given in order to equip Lewis and Clark with the most basic GPS system that you can buy in Wal-Mart for $249? What would Pierpont Morgan have paid for the worst middle seat in coach class on the evening flight from New York to London—so that he could work a full day on Wall Street, then work the next full day at his offices in Princes Gate, and then fly back to New York that second night? (In his day, the round trip consumed 10 days at sea.) How many more defining discoveries might Einstein have made if he owned the same scientific calculator which cost you less than $100?

Thus, the commoditization of miracles—which breeds the unconscious assumption that the really big breakthroughs are behind us, that however exponential progress has been so far, from here on out it'll be essentially linear. In other words, *people seem intuitively to think progress is slowing down, when in fact it is quite obviously speeding up.*

I may have seemed to be kidding, in earlier chapters, about nanotechnology as a candidate for the next great "new era" bubble. But in fact, between 2010 and 2025, nanotechnology (especially in its medical applications) is probably going to be the big technological story. And once again, the most surprising thing will be that people are surprised.

Geopolitically, the world always appears to be going to hell in a handbasket, when in fact it is demonstrating progress on a scale hitherto unimaginable. When I was born, the world was in the grip of a global conventional war, which lasted six years and one day—from September 1, 1939, when Hitler invaded Poland, to September 2, 1945, when the Japanese signed the instrument of surrender. That war killed, directly or indirectly, 55 million people, or about 26,000 war dead per day.

This was followed by 40 years of nuclear and then thermonuclear standoff between the forces of totalitarian communism and those of democratic capitalism. There came a morning in October 1962 when I sat in an economics class at Columbia University, looking out the window at a heartstoppingly beautiful autumn day, wondering if I would be able to see the thermonuclear explosion that was going to kill me. I didn't take it personally, because I knew that if I died, everyone in New York, and perhaps most of the human species, was going to die as well. For this was the Cuban Missile Crisis, and it was as close as humankind ever came to destroying itself.

The world didn't end that day, but the balance of terror defined geopolitics for more than another quarter century, until—on November 9, 1989—the Berlin Wall was torn down, and the modern world was born. Capitalism vanquished socialism that night—and it has been sweeping the globe ever since. Today, even in a totalitarian communist state like China, and a sclerotic socialist state like India, free enterprise is the defining impulse, and it is pulling tens of millions of people out of poverty every year.

(Lou Dobbs and his protectionist ilk may decry the movement of textile manufacturing jobs to China. But a so-called "trade deficit" with that country seems to me an infinitely more elegant problem than the threat—a very real threat, in my day—of an exchange of thermonuclear missiles with a society that could lose a hundred million people and not miss them.)

Today, the United States is the only remaining superpower, and its warriors are under fire in only two countries: Iraq (about the size of California) and Afghanistan. Granted, the war against terror is a genuine global war. And granted, there is genocide and unspeakable poverty in parts of Africa still ruled by criminal regimes. But relative peace and absolute prosperity are at all-time high levels in the world—and those trends are going up sharply.

Yet if the World Bank publishes a report that free-market capitalism and trade vaulted a hundred million people in China, India, Brazil and Indonesia across the poverty line last year—and on the same day a suicide bomber kills himself and nine other people in Kabul, Baghdad or Gaza City—you know which of those two stories will lead that night's newscasts.

(This is an anecdotal insight into the difficult problem of journalism. I will have more to say about the single-mindedly corrosive effects of journalism on investor psychology when we get to the chapters on bear markets. For the moment, suffice it to say that if history must make optimists of us all, journalism can make a pessimist out of almost anyone on any given day—by isolating on, and extrapolating, the apocalypse *du jour)*.

Not surprisingly, the prosperity of the world's richest, deepest, most entrepreneurial, most productive, most flexible, most transparent capitalist economy—ours—has advanced, in my lifetime, as never before. And the equity values of its great companies have more than kept pace. On the day I was born—Monday, October 11, 1943—the Standard & Poor's stock index closed at 12. As I write, it's 1200—but that, of course, ignores dividends. So although stock prices—assuming the dividends were spent—may have appreciated a hundred times, if you add back the dividends, and compound them, the growth in my lifetime is closer to a thousand times.

While it was accomplishing this unprecedented accretion of real wealth, the American equity market went down an average of almost 30% on 13 separate occasions. After each of these episodes—all of which were reported by journalism as The End Of Economic Life On The Planet As We Have Known It—economic expansion resumed, and the long-term uptrend in equity values followed suit. This forces the reasonable observer to conclude that the advance of American economic and financial success is permanent, while the cyclical downturns which punctuate it are temporary.

All of which—the long-term medical/scientific, technological and economic/financial truth—is meant to demonstrate just one thing: *optimism—what I choose to call "faith in the future"—is the only realism.* Long-term pessimism—or what I'll call declinism—is, on the other hand, deeply counterintuitive.

No one examining the record of humankind, and especially the record in our lifetimes, would arrive logically at a declinist conclusion. You'd have to read into the future something which has no historical basis or precedent. You'd have to subscribe to the particular and peculiar mental illness which manifests itself in the insistence that *"This time is different."*

Just before summarizing in a single sentence the whole concept of active, abiding faith in the future, let me offer you a practice management tip which may save you thousands of hours, and heaven knows how much heartache, over the course of your advisory career. Simply stated, *you will never make a good investor out of someone who is fundamentally afraid of the future.*

I'm certainly not suggesting that you can't get him to invest in equities: you can and you will, especially when the market is making new highs. What I'm telling you is that you won't be able to *keep* him in the market: when it goes down—and especially when it goes down a lot—this will confirm all his primal pessimistic biases, and he will panic out. "Do not try to teach a mule to dance," said Mark Twain. "It wastes your time, and upsets the mule." Know your client; pick your battles. We do behavior modification, not psychotherapy.

And now, as promised, the essential epiphany of true, long-term faith in the future, stated as an affirmation:

"I CAN'T KNOW EXACTLY **HOW** THINGS ARE GOING TO TURN OUT ALL RIGHT.

"I JUST KNOW **THAT** THINGS ARE GOING TO TURN OUT ALL RIGHT."

If you can say that mantra, and really believe it, you're going to be a great long-term investment advisor. Because you've discovered the essence of how the capital markets in the world's greatest free economy actually work.

4

SUMMARY

⸙ The portfolio management philosophy of the BIC calls for the concentration of time and energy on variables which (a) can to some very great extent be controlled, and (b) have the most pronounced effect on long-term, real life returns.

⸙ This book maintains that there are six such variables: three *principles* grounded in the belief system of the investor, and three *practices* carried out within the portfolio itself.

⸙ The principles are much more important than the practices—indeed they dictate the practices, just as belief always dictates behavior.

⸙ Faithful maintenance of the three principles as cardinal tenets of one's investment belief system, and consistent execution of the three practices, will probably drive something like 90% of long-term, real-life portfolio return. Selection and timing therefore might—and I say again *might*—govern the remaining ten percent.

⸙ The first and greatest of the principles is *faith in the future*: the belief, based solidly on the historical record, that optimism is the only realism. Optimism is the only conclusion supported by the facts. The commoditization of miracles—that is, the almost instant progress of anything from breakthrough to commonplace—blinds us to the fact that progress is not linear, but exponential, and that in fact the curve of the exponent is bending upwards.

⸙ A soccer mom's minivan contains multiples of all the computing power that was available to NASA in 1970, on the night the Apollo 13 blew up. Since that night, computing power has gotten a million times smaller, a million times cheaper, and a thousand times more powerful. This is a billionfold increase in computing power per dollar. In about the next quarter century, another such billionfold leap will take place; when it's done, information technology will have solved all our problems, including—but certainly not limited to—energy, poverty, disease and the environment.

§ Long-term pessimism, on the other hand, is not merely wrong but counterintuitive: no one examining history—and especially the last half-dozen decades—would arrive at a fundamentally declinist worldview.

§ Faith in the future announces itself with a mantra: "I don't know exactly *how* things will turn out all right; I just know *that* they will turn out all right."

SIX STEPS TO THE UPPER REACHES
PART 2

WE PROCEED NOW TO THE SECOND OF THREE GREAT attitudinal/behavioral steps which must, together with the three portfolio practices which follow, carry our clients to the upper reaches of long-term, real-life investment outcomes.

This quality is so important that it outranks all other behavioral values *except faith in the future*, to which it runs a fairly close second. It is most noteworthy in that it is, today, surely the most un-American of values—antithetical not only to the 24/7 trading culture which has largely supplanted the idea of long-term investing, but to our entire instant-gratification, charge-it-to-your-credit-card, no-payments-'til-October culture itself. This value is, of course:

2. PATIENCE. We live not in an age of enduring investment truths but of late-breaking market news, and this places the investor under constant pressure to do *something*—to react to the events of the moment rather than acting on the goals of his lifetime and beyond.

Yet the more the investor gives in to the fads or fears of the moment—the more he chases what's hot, and eschews what's not—the more he loses sight of his long-term financial goals, the more mistakes he makes, and the more his long-term return declines.

The University of California scholars Brad Barber and Terrance Odean demonstrated some years ago—in a paper with the popular title of "Trading Is Hazardous To Your Wealth"—that the more often investors changed their portfolios, the lower their returns went. (They also discovered that the things people sold did better than the things they bought with the proceeds of the sales.)

Some time later, the great behavioral economist Richard Thaler and his colleague Shlomo Benartzi found that the more often people even *looked at* their portfolios, the lower their returns—apparently because, the more often you price your portfolio, the more likely you are inopportunely to ditch something that appears to be lagging and to go chasing something that's currently shooting the lights out.

(This is only logical: inasmuch as price and value are always and everywhere inversely related, selling the high-value/low-priced laggard to buy the low-value/high-priced "winner" must surely be a formula for substandard returns. That's the ultimate irony inherent in performance-chasing.)

But changing their investments more often than most people change the sheets is not the only way in which investors exhibit impatience with long-term, goal-focused portfolio strategies. Another is drawing long-term conclusions from short- to intermediate-term data. At the end of 2002—just after one of the greatest equity market bottoms any of us will ever see, if not *the* greatest—it was fashionable to cite the factoid that, for the last five years, bonds had outperformed equities. They could hardly not have done so.

The impatient mistake prompted by that statistical snippet would, of course, have been twofold: (a) deciding that bonds' long-term return would now continue to be higher than that of equities, which is certainly counterintuitive and may even, given an efficient market, be impossible; and (b) fundamentally altering one's long-term stocks/bonds asset mix *when one's long-term goals—chief among which must be a retirement income one doesn't outlive—had not changed at all.*

Another aspect of impatience is the oft-quoted objection that "I haven't made any money" in equities in the *"X"* number of years since some epic market peak. This remained a hugely popular manifestation well into 2008, with reference to the great bubble top in 2000. And it was narrowly true…if you didn't count dividends. But it conveniently ignored the fact that, in the seven years *before* that bubble top, the equity market had nearly quadrupled.

Finally, of course, the greatest test of patience is when the equity market—and one's account values—are going down, and won't stop. During such episodes, "impatience" may seem (and indeed may be) an understatement in describing investor emotions. But it is at just such times that investors—even those who don't lose faith—simply lose patience: "I can get a 5% guaranteed return while this market is behaving so insanely, and I'm just going to go do it, until the market regains its senses."

The speaker of this seemingly common-sense statement will probably not have noticed, in his impatience, that he has now obligated himself to call the equity market right *not once but twice.* For not only does he have to be right that it isn't too late to get out—that the market still has a lot farther to fall—*but he's also going to have to get back in right* (that is, far enough down from here to make the whole exercise worth it). Few people can ever do this, and absolutely no one can do it consistently.

The fact that the markets aren't doing what you want them to do—when you want them to do it—is not an indictment of the markets. Nor is it an intelligent basis for significant changes in your investment policy, much less in your portfolio. It (or the degree of your vexation with it) is nothing more than a focal point for your own inappropriate impatience.

All you can ask of your asset allocation model and your portfolio composition is (1) that they are appropriate to the realization of your long-term financial goals in that (2) they have historically resulted over time in returns which can adequately fund your goals. *You cannot ask them to be doing those things all the time,* because they just won't.

How you react—or, much more accurately: *how you keep yourself from reacting*—to even protracted periods when your asset/portfolio mix seems to have gone off the beam is the acid test of your capacity for patience, and thus a key determinant of your long-term, real-life return.

In the last chapter, we saw the essential epiphany of faith in the long-term future expressed as an affirmation: "I can't know exactly *how* it's going to turn out all right; I just know *that* it's going to turn out all right." As you might expect, then, the virtue of patience has its own corollary epiphany:

> "I CAN'T KNOW **WHEN** IT'S GOING TO
> TURN OUT ALL RIGHT.
>
> I JUST KNOW **THAT** IT'S GOING TO
> TURN OUT ALL RIGHT."

Just before leaving this second behavioral principle, I hope you won't mind me pointing out that, without a solid underpinning of faith in the future, the kind of patience I've described here will simply be impossible for most people. This is exactly why these two values appear in the order in which I rank them.

Which brings us to the third and last of these principles:

3. DISCIPLINE. Two of the definitions of this word which appear in my dictionary are "orderly or prescribed conduct or pattern of behavior," and "self-control." But isn't patience an important manifestation of self-control as well? Where, then, does patience

leave off and discipline begin? I'm sure I don't know, and I don't believe it's very important. But I do think the two concepts are sufficiently different, in their application to investor behavior, that they each deserve a place in the six steps to the upper reaches.

Patience, to me, is forbearance: tolerance and restraint in the face of provocation. It is the refusal of the investor to react inappropriately to disappointing events: a generalized market decline, a well-regarded portfolio manager who goes stone cold, or a protracted period of below-trendline equity market returns. Patience thus dictates a ***decision not to do something wrong*** in your long-term, goal-focused portfolio. Discipline, on the other hand, is ***the decision to keep doing the right things.***

A 53-year-old couple, their last child out of college and their mortgage paid off, begins the long run toward retirement, 10 or a dozen years hence. They are going to invest the same sums monthly in a beautifully diversified portfolio of equity funds, and harness the underappreciated but tremendously powerful force of dollar-cost averaging. They invest in Month One…and the market goes down. They barely notice; Month Two comes around quickly, their investments are debited from their checking accounts…and the market sinks again.

This goes on for three more months, with the media blaring about recession, or inflation, or the overleveraged consumer, or whatever one-variable disaster it has chosen to isolate on this month. And suddenly the folks are starting to wonder aloud if they shouldn't hold off on further contributions until "things turn around."

This is the moment when the BIC is in his glory. He knows that economic analysis and market prognostication won't save the day. If anything will, it's ***discipline:*** the decision to keep on doing the right thing. And without a BIC's empathetic, encouraging counsel, that decision will probably never be made.

Incidentally, this little fable also illustrates one of the most inappropriate—but most deeply hard-wired—tendencies we find in investors who are still in the accumulation phase of life: an aversion to falling prices. This is the exact opposite of common sense.

Someone who is a regular buyer of equities should treat lower prices as heaven-sent. They're lowering his average cost—letting him buy more and more shares with the same regular contributions—and thus almost certainly raising his prospective real-life return. The BIC says, "Not only should we keep investing regularly, we should hope things *don't* turn around anytime soon, because we want to accumulate as many bargain-priced shares as we can *before the sale ends!*"

Thus, discipline's mantra is:

> "I DON'T CARE WHAT'S WORKING NOW.
> I CARE ABOUT WHAT'S ALWAYS
> WORKED...AND I'M JUST GOING TO
> KEEP DOING WHAT'S ALWAYS WORKED."

 The undisciplined investor *reacts*—he allows his long-term investment plan to be derailed by some trend or event, and the plan thus inevitably fails. Never mind that the portfolio is at all times full of nothing but five-star funds. *When discipline fails, the plan fails.*

The disciplined investor *continues to act*, regardless of the terrors or enthusiasms of the season. And because of that relentlessly appropriate action, her plan succeeds; that is, it results in the achievement of her long-term goals. Obviously, what keeps her acting positively and consistently is the behavioral coaching of the BIC.

When did investment advisors lose their belief in these three cardinal principles? Perhaps more to the point, when did we lose our adherence to those principles as *an essential element in our value proposition*? When—assuming we were ever trained to do so in the first place, which seems at least doubtful these days—did we cease to believe in the great worth of our ability to keep people acting appropriately, as opposed to our dubious skills as economic commentators, market prognosticators or performance handicappers? *When did we decide that it was more important for us to appear smart, rather than to be genuinely good?*

Perhaps we were never offered the choice. Or we were, and we didn't want it. (Certainly when I came into the business in 1967 as a stockbroker trainee, I never thought of anything beyond the ability to spot trends, trade individual stocks and generate lots of commissions.) If that's the case, I suppose I'm in danger of doing what a lot of people of a certain age do: longing for a past that never existed.

No matter: in advocating for your ability to change people's lives by hewing to these three principles—and the three practices which follow—I'm certainly offering you a better future. Think about that future—think about all the good you're going to be able to do for people *who will allow you to do it for them*—as we begin our examination of the three portfolio practices which carry the three principles into action. And the greatest of these is:

4. ASSET ALLOCATION. The timing-and-selection culture in which we live does not merely distort long-term investment reality: it stands reality on its head.

That culture maintains that portfolio return is predominately a function of which securities one owns (selection), and when (timing). It would almost have to assert this. Imagine the consequences to financial cable channels and magazines if they repeatedly acknowledged the truth: "There are half a dozen timeless principles and practices which—implemented in a goal-focused, plan-driven portfolio—must account for upwards of 90% of long-term, real-life return." In three months, they'd be out of business.

In the long run, timing and selection have very little to do with portfolio returns. A far greater determinant is *asset allocation,* which I define here as the long-term mix, in the portfolio, of stocks, bonds and cash.

There have been any number of empirical studies which document this conclusion, perhaps the most well-known of which is the 1986 paper "Determinants of Portfolio Performance" by Gary Brinson, L. Randolph Hood and Gilbert Beebower (*Financial Analysts Journal*, July/August 1986). Without belaboring the methodology (which you are welcome and even urged to examine for yourself), the "Brinson study," as it's come to be known, asserted that, on average, a portfolio's static target asset allocation accounted for some 93% of its variation in returns and volatility. The other 7% came from timing, selection, and everything else other than asset allocation.

Clearly, you don't need to buy into the numerical conclusion (93%/7%) in order wholeheartedly to embrace the conceptual conclusion: over an investing lifetime, the big swing in portfolio returns comes from what percentage of your holdings was in equities. This is only logical. All you have to do is look at the yawning chasm between the long-term returns of equities and those of bonds to see that it must be true.

AVERAGE ANNUAL COMPOUND RETURNS 1926–2007

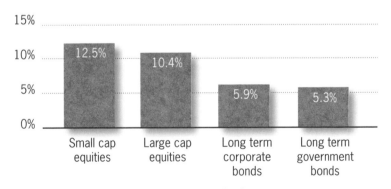

Source: ©2008 Morningstar. All rights reserved. Used with permission.

And these are just nominal returns, which really don't mean very much to the long-term investor, whose most deadly financial enemy is the erosion of purchasing power. Net out 3% CPI inflation over the period in the chart above, and the gap in real returns becomes even more pronounced:

AVERAGE ANNUAL COMPOUND RETURNS 1926–2007
NET OF CPI INFLATION

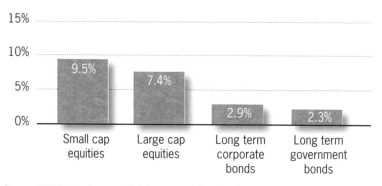

Source: ©2008 Morningstar. All rights reserved. Used with permission.

Thus, although it looked at first glance as if the blended return of large and small equities was pushing twice that of bonds, in real terms—that is, in the only terms that truly matter—the equity premium is much greater, indeed closer to three times.

Again, ***this is only logical.*** (The capital markets can, and often will, be insane in the short run. They cannot be anything but logical in the long run.) The premium return of equities is an efficient market's way of pricing in the volatility (i.e. the unreliability) of those returns. The volatility of bonds' return is much less than that of equities, and they therefore return much less. That's the package. That's the deal.

There are, therefore, no such things as "good stock markets" and "bad stock markets." There is only ***one efficient market***, in which prices may be rising or falling during any given season, but which is always doing the same thing: ***providing significantly greater real long-term returns than bonds because of its significantly greater*** *volatility*, defined here as the extreme variability of returns over the short to intermediate term.

What is most noteworthy about this ironbound relationship is the permanent nature of the premium return, and the temporary nature of negative volatility. As I pointed out earlier, equity prices have risen roughly a hundred times in my lifetime (with dividends reinvested, total return is close to a thousand times). But during that period—as we will see in graphic detail in the chapters on bear markets—there have been a baker's dozen bear episodes (declines of roughly 20% or more on a closing basis). The average of these 13 ends of the world (for as such they were reported in the media) was very nearly 30%.

What does that tell you? Precisely this: *that a free market advances permanently even as it occasionally contracts cyclically.* I suggested in the last chapter that faith in the future, far from being a hope held in spite of the facts, was the only empirically available worldview. By now I hope you're beginning to see why.

The more people are left alone to act in their own best interests—to buy, sell, form businesses, hire, fire, trade, consume, save, and invest for the betterment of themselves and their families—the more the global economy must expand, and become more efficient. And in the long run, free capital markets—and especially the equity market—*can only reflect this*. Why are equity prices up something like 70 times since the end of WWII? Because corporate earnings are up about 70 times. *It could not—other than cyclically, temporarily—be otherwise.*

So at this point you should be connecting three fundamental ideas. The first is that, in the long run, equity markets must accurately reflect the earnings, cash flows and dividends of the publicly held businesses in the underlying economy—that "the stock market" is not a casino, and not a game to be played, but a relentlessly efficient way of discounting the future earnings of real businesses.

Second, the earnings, cash flows and dividends of thriving companies must and do reflect the growth of the domestic and global economies in which they operate—growth which waxes at some times and wanes at others *around a secularly rising trendline*, which itself reflects an increasingly free (and therefore increasingly vibrant) global economy.

Third, because of the volatility of the business, credit and market cycles, equity returns are so much less certain than those of bonds that an efficient market demands of the equity market premium long-term returns as compensation. This premium return has been—in real terms, over the last eight decades or so—around three times the real return of bonds. (Another way to look at equities is in relation to inflation itself. Jeremy Siegel, in the perennial classic book *Stocks for the Long Run,* puts this premium at about 700 basis points over inflation *going back to 1802*.)

This final point must lead us to conclude that the premium returns and the premium volatility of equities are a kind of equation: they're two sides of the same coin, and you get the return only by accepting the volatility. (There is a phrase for trying to get one without the other: market timing…the ultimate no-no.)

This is a critical element in the BIC's training of his clients. She conditions them not just to accept volatility but to embrace it, because it's where the premium returns are coming from. An investor who needs and wants the lifetime returns of equities—both compared to inflation and compared to bonds—would never wish volatility away, because he would be wishing the premium return away. You don't want that. *You want your volatility.*

Take all the time you need, in order to get your mind wrapped around this idea. All successful investing is a battle between one's need for certainty and one's tolerance for ambiguity. The emotional capacity to function under uncertainty is both the key to capturing equity returns and a critical test of one's emotional maturity.

The more certainty you need, the more you'll allocate your portfolio toward bonds, and the lower your lifetime total return will be. The more ambiguity you can tolerate, the more you'll trust your fortune to equities—even, and especially, when you have no idea why they're doing what they're doing—and the higher your lifetime return will be.

Once again, therefore, we see that successful investing isn't intellectual, but emotional/behavioral. And why the advice of a Behavioral Investment Counselor—rather than an economic and market prognosticator or an advanced disciple of Modern Portfolio Theory—is truly indispensable to a lifetime of superior returns.

SUMMARY

  The second governing principle of three—so important that only faith in the future outweighs it—is ***patience***.

  Assaulted remorselessly by 24/7 cable and internet "news," the hapless investor is constantly made to feel that he ought to do ***something***. Yet the more often one changes one's portfolio—indeed, there's evidence that the more often one even looks at one's portfolio—the lower will be the return.

  An important corollary is that fundamentally changing one's portfolio when one's long-term goals have not changed is virtually always wrong, and will depress returns.

  This is most glaringly true in the decision to get out of the equity market, with the intention of getting back in at a "better time." In order to do this successfully, you have to be right twice. You won't be. Buffett: "The stock market is a highly efficient mechanism for the transfer of wealth from the impatient to the patient."

  The mantra of patience: "I don't know when it's going to turn out all right. I just know that it's going to turn out all right."

  Discipline is the third and final principle. If patience is tolerance and restraint in the face of provocation—the decision not to do something wrong—discipline is more properly the decision to keep doing the right things. Persisting in one's accumulation program is one common, and all too rare, manifestation of discipline.

  Discipline's mantra: "I don't care what's working now; I care about what's always worked, and I'm going to persist in doing the things that have, most reliably, always worked."

§ The first of the three fundamental portfolio practices is ***asset allocation***, used here simply to mean the long-term mix of stocks, bonds and cash—most particularly the first two of these. (So-called tactical asset allocation—frequent and significant changes in the mix, either in anticipation of or in reaction to market trends—is simply market-timing by a euphemistic name.)

§ That the stock/bonds mix must dominate all other elements of portfolio return is intuitive: the 80-odd-year nominal return of equities is pushing twice that of bonds, and net of inflation is closer to three times.

§ The difference between equity and bond returns is a function of equities' much greater volatility—the relative unpredictability, over shorter periods, of their return. But, as we shall see in much greater detail in the chapters on bear markets, volatility isn't risk to the long-term investor. And, in an efficient market, premium equity returns are only available due to premium equity volatility.

SIX STEPS TO THE UPPER REACHES
PART 3

THE SECOND OF THREE PORTFOLIO PRACTICES
which the BIC employs to carry our three behavioral principles
into action is:

5. DIVERSIFICATION. We noted, in our discussion of the three
principles, that patience was of such huge importance in a behavioral approach to investing that only faith in the future takes prece-
dence over it. In just the same sense, diversification—unwaveringly
disciplined diversification—is so critical to long-term investment
success that it stands second only to asset allocation. And it is very
different therefrom: asset allocation speaks to the stocks/bonds/
cash mix, while diversification suggests a portfolio approach **within one asset class**. (This is a very important distinction, and must
not, in your conversations with investors, be permitted to blur.)

Diversification is perhaps the easiest investment concept to understand and the hardest to practice, because it is, in its essence,
institutionalized ambiguity. It is studied, passionate uncertainty,
worn almost as a badge of honor.

Equity diversification says: we can't know what sectors—small or large cap, growth or value, domestic or international—are going to be hot next, nor which will fade for a season or two. So we will own a number of such opposing sets, in roughly equal measure. Because they are all equities, we will ultimately get equities' blended long-term return. But because they run on different cycles—some shooting the lights out while others lie dormant, then suddenly reversing roles—the full volatility of the equity cycle may be somewhat blunted at any given moment.

Note that, for purposes of the point we're making, there is no difference between bullish certainty—"It's a new era! Let's put all our money into calls on the nanotechnology ETF on margin!"—and bearish certainty—"It's the end of the world; the sky is falling; let's put all our money in Treasury bills!" The resulting underdiversification is only the symptom; *the disease is certainty.* (And when certainty becomes almost universal, you are always, *always* near a major market turning point, because huge consensus is always, always wrong.)

Disciplined equity diversification—a portfolio that remains spread across several styles which run counter to each other—is thus uncertainty enshrined. And it is virtually a pact with heaven:

> "I WILL NEVER OWN ENOUGH OF ANY ONE THING TO BE ABLE TO MAKE A KILLING IN IT.

> "I WILL NEVER OWN ENOUGH OF ANY ONE THING TO BE ABLE TO GET KILLED BY IT."

Incidentally, I suspect that the last six Ivy League Ph.D. theses on diversification, reduced to their purest essence, would sum to these same 35 words. And the more you look deeply into that trade-off, the more luminous it becomes. Because, in protecting the investor from the siren song of certainty, disciplined diversification—like all these principles and practices—is protecting him from himself. It is doing this by insulating him from his deep, all-too-human desire to bet the ranch on any one idea, be it a "new era" or Armageddon.

Diversification does not necessarily imply owning everything. (That's closer to indexing.) It means owning things that are essentially opposites. When my growth portfolios are on a real tear, as they were in the dying days of the great 1982–2000 bull market, my value portfolios will tend to be languishing, if not swooning. (Let it never be forgotten that Berkshire Hathaway, perhaps the ultimate value stock, made its cyclical low on the very same day Nasdaq made its all-time high.)

Small cap tends to really roar after big cap has been bid up so far that the smart money can no longer find any value in the latter, which then underperforms. International/emerging markets tend significantly to outperform domestic U.S. equities (in this increasingly interconnected global market) primarily when they're getting a lot of help from a falling dollar. The converse is also true: a strong dollar cheapens earnings in other currencies, and makes U.S. equities seem to be doing that much better.

That's my idea of diversification: deliberately attempting to create some tensions within an equity portfolio by owning sets of things that usually run on different cycles. Again, I'm going to end up with the blended long-term return of all the components, but the whole portfolio should never be diving (or soaring, for that matter) in formation, like the Blue Angels. Thus, my default, and even bonehead, portfolio might look, in equal amounts, like this:

BIG CAP GROWTH   BIG CAP VALUE
SMALL CAP GROWTH   SMALL CAP VALUE
INTERNATIONAL/EMERGING MARKETS

Why not midcap, you ask? My answer is a question: what runs counter to it? What does midcap naturally pull against, so that we could say that when midcap is "working," another sector usually isn't? I confess I've never been able to find an answer to that question (which certainly doesn't suggest that you can't), and on that basis, I pass.

There is also the issue, for me, of just owning too much...*stuff*. If I don't think that portfolio composition accounts for a very big part of long-term, real-life return—and this whole book cries out that I don't—then elaborate, multi-faceted portfolios are just naturally going to make my eyes glaze over.

I have a pretty low threshold of boredom to begin with, and nuanced quantitative analysis of a sixth, seventh, eighth or (God help us) ninth fund for my portfolio just doesn't seem like a good use of my time. I could be taking Rebecca and Will to a museum, or holding hands with my bride while she tells me the names of the stars in the Big Dipper. Or something.

What's that? There isn't enough international exposure in there? Again, my answer is a question: are you sure? And here's my follow-up question: are you wanting to get more exposed to foreign *stock markets* or to foreign *businesses*? Because they're not at all the same thing.

If I own stock in Goldman Sachs, Coca-Cola, Caterpillar, Pfizer, Intel and Apple, is my portfolio 100% domestic? Of course not: half the revenue and earnings streams that I own are coming from offshore. And that, of course—not where the companies are headquartered, still less where the stocks are traded—is my test of the extent to which my portfolio is overseas. In this example, I'm something like 50%/50%.

Follow that train of thought to its logical conclusion. In my bonehead five-fund portfolio (or five-SMA portfolio, or five-sub-account portfolio, or whatever), I've got 20% of my money in each of big cap value and big cap growth, right? OK, assume that my big cap companies are doing even 40% of their business overseas. There's 16% foreign exposure, right there (i.e. 40% of my portfolio gets 40% of its revenues offshore).

Now say that my small cap accounts (the next 40% of my total portfolio) have even 15% offshore revenue streams. That's another six percent of my total portfolio revenues. Added to the 16% from the big cap accounts, I'm now getting 22% of my revenues/earnings from foreign lands.

Finally, in fairness, assume that my last portfolio component—the 20% I've got in nominally foreign funds—does, say, 30% of its business in the U.S. The other 70%, *or 14% of my whole portfolio*, is generated overseas.

Don't look now, but that means my portfolio is invested 36% in foreign *businesses*…even though I only have 20% of my equity holdings in foreign *markets*. That's plenty, for me. And I'm betting that it's plenty for most other Americans, *who don't want to take a shot at making a killing (overseas, in this case) if that carries with it the risk that they'll get killed*. Play with the above numbers all you like. You may end up with different percentages. But I strenuously doubt that you'll come to a very different philosophical conclusion.

Do you want to go back to my bonehead five-point portfolio, and layer an institutional quality REIT in there, to the tune of maybe 10% of the total portfolio? Knock yourself out; you'll get no argument from me. Operating real estate has historically been a powerful diversifier in a portfolio of financial assets. That's because (again, *historically*) real estate has correlated positively with inflation, while stocks and bonds have correlated negatively with it.

Besides, people just *like* real estate (even if it's for the wrong reasons), and it may help them feel better to know that their portfolio is anchored in something that seems to them more solid (i.e. less quixotic) than "the stock market."

In the end, I'm much less interested in *how* you're diversified than I am in the fact *that* you're meaningfully diversified, *and that you stay that way, regardless of the fads or fears of the moment*. (If you suddenly found yourself getting all excited as you read the hypothetical portfolio specifics above, and you started thinking about how you might modify or tweak them to make the portfolio "perform" even better, it's a sure sign that you have missed the point. To be precise, it suggests that the highly addictive drug *selection* is still flooding your synapses—and that drug is a very hard habit to break.) I suggested a model diversified portfolio only because I didn't think I could get away with not doing so—much as I might have liked to.

What about diversifying out of mainstream equities altogether: into hedge funds, managed futures programs, and private equity funds? Here again, I must confess a bias, as much as or more than I'm stating a principle: I just don't see the need. And I do see the dangers.

I freely acknowledge that huge, putatively sophisticated institutions— Harvard's and Yale's endowment funds, a state pension fund, an immensely wealthy family foundation—may find some incremental value in such adventures. (I do not claim to know how. The operative verb form I used was "*may* find" incremental value; I accept this possibility only because I haven't a firm basis on which to reject it.)

But I cannot see that the retail investor and his family—even people who enjoy significant net worth—need such additional exposure, nor can I believe that they will understand what they own if they do. (Damned few investors I've ever encountered in 40-plus years in this profession understand the mainstream equity market, for that matter.) And the less the investor understands what he owns, the more likely he is to bail out of it at exactly the wrong moment, when it heels over in a gale, and just before it rights itself.

There is, finally, the question of exactly what *you* can claim to know about these more exotic arrangements. I was once asked with great sincerity by a very conscientious advisor whether managed commodity funds had a place in a well-diversified portfolio. My answer was both simple and Socratic: "Do you know anything about managed commodities?" He assured me, almost in horror, that he did not. I therefore opined that he had answered his own question: that if he wasn't pretty sure he could effectively counsel a client family about a particular investment in all the phases of its cycle, then they ought not to own it—or at least not through him. This is, in its essence, my counsel to you. Diversification almost for its own sake—or because it is the fashion of a particular season—in enterprises that are significantly more exotic than mainstream equities ought to be undertaken with great trepidation. And it should probably be avoided altogether, unless you and your client are absolutely convinced (a) that it is genuinely necessary to the efficient functioning of the overall portfolio, and (b) *that you both completely understand it*. Much more often than not, in your career, I think you'll find that most exotic investment media will fail one or both of these tests.

In enumerating the manifold joys of equity diversification *practiced as the acquisition of sets of opposites*, let me not fail to point out a particular benefit of this strategy to the long-term accumulator (which most of us, for the 30 to 40 years of our working/saving lives, are).

Even if, as in the bonehead portfolio on page 87, one is investing exactly 20% of his capital—monthly, annually, *regularly*—in each of the five accounts, the net effect is quite a bit smarter than it may initially appear. When one set of opposites—growth and value, say—is dancing its contrapuntal minuet, one will usually be significantly "outperforming" the other. (This is exactly the point at which the average American investor, unaided by a BIC, will sell the "laggard"—just before it turns up—to chase the hot dot, just before it flames out.)

The disciplined diversifier may be investing exactly the same number of dollars in both styles, *but he is always acquiring relatively more shares of the low-price/high-value sector, even as he is buying relatively few shares of the high-price/low-value sector.* In the long run, therefore, he will always own disproportionately large numbers of shares in all his funds at below-average prices. Which means—wonder of wonders—that he will have captured, in all his funds, above-average returns. *Thus, by investing the same amounts regularly, the disciplined diversifier actually outperforms his own funds.*

I need hardly add, I hope, that when two sectors do a role-reversal—when growth, for example, takes a nap and value jumps up and shoots out every light in the joint—the disciplined diversifier immediately steps up his **share** purchases of the newly out-of-favor sector, and cuts way back on his **share** purchases of the new flavor of the month. It's automatic. There's no conscious thought involved of a timing nature. There's just the persistent, continuous, and utterly glorious operation of disciplined diversification.

A cautionary note: as delightful as the effects of systematic investing surely are, one invests over time because one must, not because one chooses to do so. That is, an accumulator is usually investing out of her earnings over years and decades, and thus is effectively forced to enjoy the benefits I've just described.

But one should never hold back, and dribble into equities over time, a lump sum. This is a loser's game. It may appear to be caution and prudence—refusing to throw a big bonus, settlement, legacy or whatever into the market all at once—but it is in fact a terrible bet against frightening odds. And the chances are overwhelmingly that it will produce far worse returns than will instant investment of the whole sum.

This is simply because the U.S. equity market has, at least since the end of WWII, gone up more than 75% of the time—indeed, very nearly four years out of five. So to withhold cash from the market is, albeit unconsciously, to bet that you're going into that one down year. The odds are upwards of four to one against this strategy producing a better outcome than investing it all by nightfall. Statistically, the only right time to invest money that ultimately has to go into equities is today.

How, then, to construct the diversified portfolio? If one chooses to invest passively—exchanging the possibility of outperforming the relevant indexes for the certainty of not underperforming them—the decision is essentially made for you, and you will select index funds and/or ETFs that suit your purposes. If, on the other hand, you feel that active management—stock-picking against the indexes, in essence—is desirable and appropriate for some or all of your portfolios, then you have your work cut out for you.

I suppose that I must stop here, to repeat and even amplify the point I made in Chapter 1: that I regard either decision as honorable. I respect the decision to index, which is (or ought to be) based on two simple premises: (1) that most active managers cannot consistently select sufficiently mispriced stocks to overcome the incremental costs of their management, and (2) that the minority of active managers who *will* outperform are not systematically identifiable before the fact.

I equally respect the decision to seek active management for some or even all of a portfolio, also essentially based on two theses. (1) That one cannot *statistically/scientifically* identify superior managers does not mean they can't be identified at all. (2) All indexes are not created equal. The thinner and/or less efficiently researched a sector is—microcap and emerging markets, for example—the greater the opportunity to select against its index.

For the purposes of this book, the active/passive debate is utterly moot, and the Behavioral Investment Counselor is indifferent to it. The philosophy we're developing here holds that the investor cannot possibly succeed or fail based on whether his portfolio is active, or passive, or both. Once more, with feeling: *the dominant determinant of long-term, real-life return is not investment performance, but investor behavior*. The advisor who gets sucked down into the active/passive debate is asserting, if only unconsciously, that selection matters critically. Every line of this book cries out that it does not.

Of the selection process for active managers—if and to the extent that that's your decision—we can only know for sure that it can't be done scientifically: that future performance cannot be inferred mathematically from past performance. That said, I can suggest a few criteria which you may wish to consider.

(A) CHARACTER. If this attribute feels diffuse and difficult to quantify, (1) it certainly is, but (2) let me narrow its contextual scope for you. I'm simply talking about the consistency of a manager in sticking to his stated discipline, even (and especially) when his discipline isn't "working."

The essence of effective diversification, as we've seen, is tension between opposing sets of management styles. The last thing you want, therefore, is accounts which, in content or style, start migrating toward each other. Thus, the mortal enemy of successful diversification isn't "underperformance," whatever the hell that means. *It's style drift.* The courageous manager will stick to his discipline, and thus his portfolio will not abandon its post in your plan.

(B) EXPERIENCE. There, I've said it: I'm older, and I have a bias for older people. They don't necessarily have to be as old as I am; indeed, who is, these days? But I breathe a little easier when I see some grey hair, some bullet holes, and some scar tissue—people with enough time in grade to have managed money through at least one bubble and one crash.

Moreover, I prefer people who've been managing their current portfolio for a good long time—as opposed to having bounced from place to place. There's experience, and then there's experience: somebody who's had five jobs in 20 years is probably a different (and not superior) breed of cat compared to someone who's had two…or even one.

Finally, I have a bias for managers whose personal wealth is invested in their own funds, or at the very least in their own fund families.

(C) LOW TURNOVER. Not just relative to her peers: I'm looking for low turnover, period. I'm a long-term (nay, multigenerational) investor, and I have a bias for professional low-turnover managers. (And the converse: being neither a speculator nor a trader, I prefer not to have my capital traded or speculated with.) It should go without saying that a low-turnover strategy tends, everything else being equal, to hold costs down—increasing the chance that the manager will "outperform," if that still floats your boat.

(D) A GOOD LONG-TERM RECORD. Here I certainly *do* mean a good record relative to his peers, not to "the market," which may or may not be an appropriate benchmark. Note that I place this issue last. This is no accident.

———

This is all, and indeed much more than, I care to say about the selection of active managers. If, again, it feels painfully unscientific to you, there is at least some hope that you've gotten the point, and therefore that you may be saved from a career of trying (and failing) to infer future performance from past performance. This approach simply enables the BIC to say:

> *"These are the managers with whom I work.*
>
> *"I do so not because they have 'outperformed' all their peers, nor as a statement that they will 'outperform' going forward.*
>
> *"Rather, it's because I know them—personally, in many or most cases—and because I trust them to be disciplined stewards of my clients' wealth.*
>
> *"Each has a consistent philosophy, and each applies it with real flair, in my judgment.*
>
> *"They have tended, over longer periods of time, to produce better (or just: more consistent) results than did most similar managers, relative to the amount of risk they took."*

The question that you who aspire to the status of BIC need to ask yourself is not what more you might be able to say, but why you would ever perceive a need to say more, and why you would ever want to.

6. REBALANCING. The sixth and final step to the upper reaches

of real-life returns—that is, the third and last of our portfolio practices—is rebalancing of the portfolio, back to the originally desired weightings, annually on the same date.

Particularly in wild bull markets—which invariably tend to narrow as they rise, so that fewer and fewer concepts/ideas/sectors are still "working"—there will come to be an unavoidable overweighting in your portfolios of those few last bubble concepts. For example, near the top of the tech bubble in late 1999, my bonehead five-account portfolio would have been something like 60% in growth, with most of that in unseasoned and highly speculative small cap growth.

Annual rebalancing on the same day—taking the portfolio back to its desired long-term composition—has the effect of withdrawing capital from the most popular/highest-priced/lowest-potential sectors and redeploying it into the out-of-favor/lower-priced/higher-potential sectors of the portfolio. (If all investing is ultimately value investing, then rebalancing may be—if only for one day a year—the ultimate value investor.)

Again: this is virtually the exact opposite of what most investors do with most of their money most of the time. Thus, something as prosaic and seemingly unimaginative as rebalancing will unfailingly (everything else being equal) cause the disciplined rebalancer to secure a better return than do the huge preponderance of other investors.

Why only once a year, and why on the same day? To the first question: because I can't find any compelling evidence that doing it more often is worth either the bother or the transaction costs, much less both. To the second: because anything and everything else is closet market timing, and therefore to be rigorously eschewed.

Being human, you may fairly often find yourself looking about the landscape and saying things like, "Hmmm. Growth (or emerging markets, or whatever) is starting to look awfully pricey in here, and (whatever else) has been dormant for these last three years (or whatever blink of an eye suddenly feels to you like a period of geologic time). Perhaps I ought to, uh, *rebalance*."

Excuse me: this is market timing, pure and simple, and to call what you're about to do "rebalancing" is like calling bank robbery "unscheduled, involuntary withdrawal of other depositors' balances." **Don't kid yourself.** It's rebalancing only if it's done at the same regular interval—as a discipline, and not as any kind of "call" on the markets.

We have come, then, to the end of our extended discussion of the six steps which must surely carry our clients into the upper reaches of long-term, real-life returns. Does someone still ask, "How far up is 'upper'?" Sorry: I still don't know…but I'm hoping that, by now, you no longer care. That is, I hope and even expect that you see in these six steps a paradigm so clear, compelling and eminently practicable that you no longer doubt your ability to build a thriving practice upon them. If I've done my job right in these three chapters, you have come to wonder not how you will ever convince your more substantial prospects of the power of the six steps, but rather how any real prospect could seriously doubt them…*or you.*

From this point forward, the book you're reading will be a series of exercises in the application of the six steps. We are, for example, just about to embark on a discussion of the classic mistakes—the lifetime return-killers which are so critical (and common) to the process by which the average fund investor regularly blows upwards of 60% of the return available from the average fund, over 20 year clips.

That being the case, you will be best served by working through the rest of the book with the three principles and three practices firmly in your mind. To that end, I strongly recommend that you stop here, go back, and read these last three chapters straight through once more. As you do so, please try to see them not as six different ideas, but as the one complete thought that they truly are.

SUMMARY

§ The second of the three key portfolio practices is ***diversification***, the spreading of risk and reward within an asset class.

§ Diversification is studied uncertainty: the proud acknowledgment that we can never consistently know which sectors are about to "outperform," and which will fade. Broad diversification eventually captures the full ride of all the sectors, but with somewhat muted volatility at any given moment.

§ Disciplined diversification is, in its essence, almost a pact with heaven: "I'll never own enough of any one thing to make a killing in it; I'll never own enough of any one thing to be able to get killed by it."

§ ***How*** you diversify is infinitely less important than ***that*** you diversify. To lose sight of this is to check back into the dungeon of selection voluntarily, and to lock yourself back in.

§ There may be an important difference between diversifying into foreign *businesses* as opposed to foreign *markets*. Be sure you understand those differences, and that you are making conscious choices.

§ "Alternative investments"—non-mainstream portfolios such as hedge funds, managed futures and private equity—should be tested by two criteria: (a) is the inclusion of such an enterprise essential to the long-term efficiency of the client's portfolio, and (b) do advisor and client alike completely understand the workings of the proposed "alternative," such that they will not be driven to bolt when it "underperforms." At least as often as not, in specific client situations, the proposed "alternative" will fail one of these key tests.

§ In the accumulation phase of his financial life, the disciplined diversifier will most often be acquiring disproportionately large numbers of shares in out-of-favor sectors—those performing below their long-term trendlines—and disproportionately small numbers of shares in "hot" sectors—those currently producing returns above their long-term trendlines. Since most of his shares in any sector will have been acquired at a below-average cost, he will enjoy, in the long run, an above-average return: that is, he will tend to outperform his own investments.

§ However, one should never withhold a lump sum from commitment to the equity market, and dribble it in over time. This always feels appropriately measured and cautious, but it is in fact a bet against daunting odds, as the equity market historically rises 75%–80% of the time. Statistically, today is the only right time to invest money that must ultimately be committed to equities.

§ Some suggested criteria for selecting active managers for long-term client portfolios: character (manifested as sticking to one's knitting and eschewing style drift), experience (with the fewer employers the better), low turnover, and a good long-term record relative to directly comparable peers.

§ Beware "overselling" individual managers. The messenger is the message: the critical variable in the client's portfolio is the presence of the BIC, not of any manager—nor of all the managers, for that matter.

§ The third practice—and therefore the sixth and last step to the upper reaches—is *rebalancing:* returning the portfolio to its target diversification annually on the same day. This will virtually always cause the sale of high-priced/low-value "hot" sectors, and the redeployment of those funds into low-priced/high-value out-of-favor sectors—the precise opposite of what most investors do. This tells you yet again how and why practitioners of the six steps almost effortlessly achieve long-term returns superior to those of their peers.

§ Doing this once a year on the same day is rebalancing. Doing it irregularly on the basis of "analysis," whim or hunch is market timing. Don't kid yourself.

§ ***Stop here.*** Go back and read the six steps all the way through again. Real slow.

PREVENTING DISASTER BEFORE IT HAPPENS: THE EIGHT GREAT BEHAVIORAL MISTAKES

LET US NOW STUDY THE MANAGEMENT OF INVEST-
or behavior by, in effect, *inverting* the previous three chapters.

It is one kind of learning experience to develop a framework for positive beliefs and behaviors—the things we and our clients must do right, in order for them to be lastingly successful investors. This is what we accomplished in those last three chapters. But it is another—and at least equally effective—learning experience *clearly to identify the major things we must not do wrong*. That's the subject of this chapter.

Scratch golfers do not necessarily hit the largest number of great shots. They hit the fewest really terrible shots. To an extent that may surprise you—and that should certainly delight you—outstanding real-life investment success proceeds from simply not making The Big Mistake. And the proclivity to make The Big Mistake—in a finite number of very predictable ways—is hard-wired into all of us.

Therefore, the Behavioral Investment Counselor can add tremendous value—can indeed earn multiples of his annual fee at critical moments—simply by dissuading his client from blowing himself up. Sometimes the greatest advice you can give a client is to say—as he's winding up to commit a classic blunder —*"You must not do that."*

This ability presumes three attributes on your part: (1) that you know what the classic mistakes are, and can observe them forming in your clients' minds; (2) that you have the courage to stand in empathetic but unshakable opposition to your clients when they want to commit these errors; and (3) that your relationships with your clients are sufficiently mature that they will turn away from these destructive behaviors *when—and simply because—you say,* *"You must not do that."*

The first of these attributes is quite easily acquired, and you will find yourself in complete mastery of it by the time you finish reading this chapter. The second will follow quickly, as you become certain that these readily identifiable manifestations of The Big Mistake are fatal to superior real-life returns.

The third one is mission critical, because if at the ultimate moment you cannot prevail on your clients to ignore the sirens' call, they will be wrecked—and your career along with them. *Giving great advice is, sadly, much less than half the battle.* Your strength of character, and the depth of your clients' trust in your behavioral advice, must be such that you are heeded. *You cannot help people who refuse—especially at critical moments—to be helped.*

What, then, are the genuinely classic, immutable, timeless human proclivities which—taken together, as one hydra-headed monster whose name is The Big Mistake—lead most reliably to the destruction of long-term, real-life return? I believe that there are eight of them. Two introductory comments about them are in order.

a. None is objectively more dangerous than another—though some are perhaps more common than others—and therefore I do not report them here in any order. Without question, *by far the most perilous of the Eight Great Mistakes is always the one that your client is winding up to make just at the moment.* So don't look to weigh, measure or calibrate them.

b. A number of the Great Mistakes can be and often are made simultaneously. That a client is busily engaged in trying to make one does not in any way immunize him against the others. Moreover, some of the Mistakes are generally made in series— euphoria giving way to panic being the most obvious of these chain reactions.

I'm hoping you realize that the names of the Great Mistakes (and even the number) can't be the critical issue, which is *knowing, training your clients, and being ever alert to the fact that there are a handful of instinctive human reactions which, left unchecked, will blow the best portfolio ever made to kingdom come.* Once again, and not for the last time: it doesn't matter what the portfolio is doing; it only matters what the investor is doing.

Here, then, are the Eight Great Mistakes:

OVERDIVERSIFICATION. You don't see this one a whole lot, and it's really an individual thing rather than a crowd phenomenon. Guy makes his 401(k) contribution annually, and every year he puts the money into the top-performing equity fund on *Forbes*'s Honor Roll. Twelve years later, he owns a hodgepodge of 12 mutual funds, because—like Miss America—nobody wins twice.

By having neither a philosophy nor a strategy for carrying it out, our friend is now the proud owner of the world's largest, least efficient, most expensive index fund—with gaps, redundancies and fee inefficiencies that would set his hair on fire if he were even remotely aware of them. By whatever methodology he gets there, the overdiversified investor, in the act of owning everything, ends up owning nothing.

UNDERDIVERSIFICATION. This one's a monster, and you usually find large swaths of the investing population trying to do it the same way at the same time. I define it as *the fatal narrowing of a portfolio down to essentially one idea.* And the more people who basically own just that one idea, the sooner all the lights go out.

In 1999, to cite a grotesque example, the premise of most Americans' stock portfolios—whether they were aware of this or not—was that Internet traffic was doubling every 100 days. It wasn't, of course, but that's irrelevant. Dot.com IPOs, e-commerce stocks, Cisco Systems at 85 times earnings and phone companies laying more fiberoptic cable than we'll use for 50 more years—all were running off this one classic misperception. (For such is the nature of all bubbles, and of all epic crashes, for that matter: they simply make up their own self-sustaining rationales as they go along.)

In the great bear market which inevitably followed, the broad equity market went down almost 50%. But the brave, resourceful, visionary tech "investor" saw Nasdaq go down 80%. And that's if he was holding his portfolio without leverage (see below). If he was on margin, or had borrowed the equity out of his McMansion to finance his stock "portfolio," he threw snake eyes. He totally zeroed out.

Then, at the classic market bottom in October of 2002 (with a reprise at the double bottom in March 2003), the portfolio of the masses once again narrowed down to one idea: Armageddon. (This time is different: they are never going to stop going down, and if by some chance they do, they are never coming back again in our lifetimes. The sky is falling. Sell at any price.) A lot of that money went into bonds, and got double whammied: it sold equities at the bottom to buy bonds at their peak, just before the interest rate cycle turned up again.

For such is the killing power of just one idea.

And, in a pinch, you don't have to buy into everybody else's one idea. You can—and uncounted numbers of "investors" do—create your own fatally underdiversified "portfolio." All you have to do is find one stock—needless to say, a stock that can only go up—and fall deeply, passionately and faithfully in love with it. You will almost certainly not notice, until it is far too late, that the stock never actually loved you back.

Holding the preponderance (much less, heaven forbid, the totality) of your equity "portfolio" in one stock isn't investing. It's Russian roulette. And every day when the market opens, you point that gun at your head and pull the trigger.

Now, your revolver may have hundreds and even thousands of empty chambers in it, such that you can go on pulling the trigger with impunity, every trading day for years and years. But the essential, overarching law of the financial universe is what the economist Joseph Schumpeter so vividly called "creative destruction."

And one fine day, my fine friend, the hammer will come down on the chamber with the bullet in it. And that will be the end of you. Blinded by love, you will have refused to see that no blue chip is so blue that it carries an exemption from the law of creative destruction. And you will pay the price.

Johns-Manville, the blue chip company that insulated every home and office in America, until we found out its insulation was a carcinogen. The mighty Penn Central Railroad, and the pioneering global airline Pan Am, whose stock actually went to zero twice. Enron, winner of *Fortune* magazine's award for the most innovative company in America *five years in a row*, until it imploded in a firestorm of fraud. Bear Stearns, the fifth largest investment banking firm in this country until, over the course of a week, it disappeared. The outstanding leaders of the first great age of computers: Burroughs, Control Data, Wang Laboratories. Blue chips all. ("One-decision stocks," they were called when I entered the profession.) Gone; all utterly gone.

In fairness, of course, maybe your own true love won't totally zero out. Maybe you'll choose a Polaroid, a Xerox or a Kodak, now selling for—what—five percent of where they were 40 years ago? How about economic stalwarts like General Motors, Ford and Chrysler? Or even Cisco, the aforementioned mother of all tech blue chips: 80 at the bubble top, then 10, and not even a third of its peak price eight years on: just the deadest of dead money. Coke: the greatest growth stock ever, and only a third off its peak eight years later. How much more of this can you stand?

I leave the topic of underdiversification in general—and overconcentrated stock positions in particular—with the immortal words of Joseph Hazelwood, captain of the ill-fated *Exxon Valdez*. Under his graduation picture in the Merchant Marine Academy yearbook appeared his motto: **"It can't happen to me."** It could, and it did. Bear this in mind. The fewer ideas in your portfolio, the fewer bullets it will take to kill you. **One idea: one bullet.**

⊘ EUPHORIA. That's what I call it, anyway. A lot of exhausted advisors, after battling it all day every day in times like 1999, simply call it greed, but I think that misses the point. To me, it's more like nitrogen narcosis—that transcendently blissful state which scuba divers call "rapture of the deep." *It's the complete loss of an adult sense of danger.*

When the euphoria hits you, you no longer fear (or even accept the possibility of) principal loss. *Your only concern is that somebody, somewhere owns stocks that are going up more than yours.* Indeed, many of us can still remember the Whine of '99: "Everybody's getting rich but me!"

A true story: an advisor friend of mine produced for one of his clients a 29% return in 1999, in a beautifully diversified, high quality equity fund portfolio. *Whereupon the client sued him.* It seems that the other three ladies with whom this client played bridge every week had averaged returns around 80%, owning heaven only knows what. The client (and her attorney, Bernie) claimed that the advisor and his firm owed her the difference.

I need hardly tell you that early in 2000, as the market imploded, the suit melted away like springtime snow. The point is that when stuff like this starts to happen, you've entered The Euphoria Zone. And at that point, as the sirens sing their song of ecstatic doom, only by keeping your clients lashed to the mast of disciplined diversification can you save them.

All new eras end in ruin, because all technological (and even financial) innovations follow the same downward arc, from miracle to commodity. (Think cell phones, personal computers and GPS.) This time is never different. Neither the business cycle nor the market cycle has ever been, or will ever be, repealed. Stand by your guns. In euphoric times, your only two choices are disciplined diversification and death.

PANIC. It is axiomatic that the biggest bear markets are simply correcting the biggest bull markets; think 1982–2000 followed by 2000–2002. The market couldn't have gone down 50% if it hadn't just finished going up 12 times; Nasdaq went down that much more because it was up that much more. (This may not compute, but it always rhymes.)

Hence, there's also a consistent relationship between the height of the mob's euphoria at the top of a big bull market and the depth of their panic-induced capitulation at the bottom of the concomitant bear. Seems obvious because it is obvious. And it explains why the same people who drank every drop of the "new era" Kool-Aid become convinced beyond a doubt, at or near epochal bottoms, that the world is coming to an end. Deal with it. By which I mean: don't let them get absurdly euphoric, because that's the only way to prevent them from abysmal capitulation.

You manage panic tomorrow by managing euphoria today. Sometime in 1997—well after Greenspan's irrational exuberance speech but still way too early—I wrote an essay in *Financial Advisor* magazine in which I said that at that point the soundness of an advisor's practice would only be known when—***not if***—the market went down 50%.

To this day, advisors still quote this back to me, in the delusional belief that I was prescient. I assure them that not only wasn't I prescient, I wasn't even particularly smart. All I am is old, and I'd seen this movie a whole bunch of times before. Believe me, the third time in your life that you see a movie about the Alamo, you're able to predict with 100% confidence that Davy Crockett is fixing to end up dead.

The world does not end; it only appears to be ending. All market declines are temporary, because the market—propelled by the economy which it reflects—is permanently rising. That is the genius of free-market capitalism, which is the most powerful idea in the globalizing economy, and the defining idea of the twenty-first century. ***This time is never different.*** I need to leave this idea here, in part because it's so transcendently obvious, and in part because bear markets are going to get two whole chapters of their own in this book a little later on.

Panic is the pure essence of a loss of faith in the future, and capitulation is a toxic weed that can only take root in optimism's dead body. If you are only just going into battle against panic, and trying to beat back clients' urge to capitulate, when blood is running in the streets (or on CNBC), you're going to lose. Indeed, you've already lost.

⊘ LEVERAGE. This is perhaps the most insidious of the Eight Great Mistakes, because one can actually make a narrow intellectual case for it when it's done right, whereas all the other seven are unthinkable on their faces.

If you thought that the long-term index return of a blended portfolio of large and small equities was anything like 10%–12%, and you could borrow on your house at 6%–7% while writing off the mortgage interest against your taxable income, there'd be a very powerful intellectual/economic case to be made for doing this. And somewhere, out of 300 million Americans, there may be as many as nine people actually doing leverage in this coldly rational way.

In practice, everybody else does it the wrong way: borrowing at the wrong times and on the wrong terms, in order to buy the wrong things at the wrong times for all the wrong reasons. I shudder to think how many people, as the year 2000 dawned, overleveraged their homes with adjustable rate debt to buy Amazon.com at 232 *on margin.*

Because they had just read *Time* magazine's Man of the Year piece on Jeff Bezos, which proclaimed—right at the tippy, tippy top—that all retailing was going to be done online, that all commerce would ultimately be e-commerce, and that grass was about to grow over all the shopping malls in America, such that only old people would one day remember where the malls had been. (It just *couldn't* be Kool-Aid—could it—if *Time* said it was Dom Perignon?)

Wrong loan, wrong terms, wrong stock, wrong time, wrong rationale: *snake eyes.* Everyone who did this zeroed out when he couldn't meet the margin calls. (Meanwhile, Amazon.com is actually doing fairly well.) When most Americans are ready to invest with their intellects, and not with their baser emotions, let me know and I'll consider taking leverage off my list of the Great Mistakes. I'm not holding my breath.

SPECULATING WHEN YOU STILL THINK YOU'RE INVESTING. And not seeing, until it's far too late, that you've gone over to the dark side. Amazon.com at the turn of the year 2000 was a good example of this Great Mistake, as well. People said, "I'm investing in e-commerce," and the tragedy is that they believed it, when they were in fact doing nothing remotely like investing.

They were buying shares in a company that had never made money—it raised equity with the stated intention of burning through it, as the business attempted to achieve scale. Moreover, the business model of which Amazon.com was a leader—e-commerce— had itself never made money, and indeed had not even existed five years earlier, because the platform on which it was being built— the Internet—was then still in its infancy. There was no assurance that the industry or the company would ever make money, much less achieve a return on capital which would justify the risk.

There is a word—a perfectly respectable word—for putting money into an enterprise such as that described in the foregoing paragraph. That word, however, is not **"investing."** It is **"speculating."** And one ought never to speculate with any part of the core capital one has committed to the achievement of the great goals of one's life. So the ability to distinguish between investment and speculation becomes critical to financial success.

All short-term trading is speculation, in that fundamental values do not change quickly. An investor is always interested in long-term improvements in earnings, cash flows and dividends. A trader is interested in quick changes in price, and is therefore always a speculator.

Similarly, all options and all futures contracts are speculations rather than investments because their ending value after expiration is zero. Therefore, buying (or selling) an option or a futures contract is a speculation on a change in the price of the underlying security or commodity, as opposed to an investment in the security's (or the commodity's) fundamental value. The common stock of Microsoft is an investment; the September 30 Microsoft call is a speculation, as is the put. Gold is an investment, though not a very good one; a futures contract for the delivery of gold in November is a speculation.

Likewise, all hedges are pure speculations, in that the creator of the hedge has no interest whatsoever in the fundamental value of the securities or commodities he's hedging: he just wants the spread to close. That is, all he cares about are prices, and specifically what the prices do in relation to each other.

Granting as one must that one hedge, one futures contract and one option are speculations not investments, there remains the question of whether professionally managed portfolios of these synthetic instruments become, by virtue of the diversification and professional management, investments. I confess that I do not have an intellectually rigorous answer to this question either way. In the next breath, let me remind you that I don't think this is the threshold question.

The critical issue is the inclusion of such funds in mainstream retail portfolios. My tests of this, as you may remember from the last chapter, are twofold. (1) Is the inclusion of a hedge fund, an options fund or a managed futures fund genuinely necessary to the efficient functioning of the overall portfolio? And (2) are you and the client both convinced that you completely understand the basic risks, rewards and strategies of the fund under consideration, such that you're both pretty sure you won't get shocked into bolting out of it at the wrong times for the wrong reasons?

I suggested in the last chapter, and now repeat, as gently as possible, that most exotic instruments—be they, finally, investments or speculations—will more often than not fail at least one of these tests in most real-world instances.

Finally, all performance-chasing—selling a fund which has lagged for the last three years to buy one which has shot out the lights—is speculating rather than investing. It is trend-following, which is the essence of speculation. It is the antithesis of a long-term investment decision, in that investment is always and everywhere the search for undervaluation, while speculation is usually the quest for price momentum.

Know the difference between speculating and investing. Do not speculate with core capital. And you can never make this Great Mistake.

INVESTING FOR CURRENT YIELD INSTEAD OF FOR TOTAL RETURN. This is the classically Great Mistake of the American retiree; indeed, it is both his art form and his tragedy. I will have so much to say about this in the chapters on a behavioral approach to retirement income investing that all we need really do here is name this Mistake, and state the essential fallacy at the heart of it.

That fallacy is based on one simple truth: investments which have the highest current yield have the lowest total return, while investments with lower current yield must—in an efficient market—compensate by offering the higher long-term total return. Since retirees' income must (a) last through three-decade retirements and (b) continually rise to offset the constantly rising cost of living, they need to focus not on today's yield but on long-term total return—that is, on both current payout *and* appreciation as potential sources of income.

The only rational test of an investment's long-term income-producing potential is its long-term total return. The total return of equities has been, over the long run, upwards of twice that of bonds. (Net of inflation, it's closer to three times.) By this one rational test, then, equities are a much more reliable source of a constantly rising income stream—one that historically far exceeds increases in the cost of living. Equities, not bonds, are thus the vastly preferable long-term income investment. **Hold that thought.**

LETTING YOUR COST BASIS DICTATE YOUR INVESTMENT DECISIONS. People just naturally—and almost always fatally—get emotionally tangled up in the price they paid for their investments. But your cost in an investment has nothing to do with its objective value today. Indeed, as I've always said, *your investments do not know what you paid for them, and would not perform any differently if they did.* Your cost is purely a suitcase of emotional baggage that you bring—or learn not to bring—to your investment decision-making process.

This behavioral boo-boo (which I've just this instant decided to christen The Cost-Basis Heuristic) most often shows up in one of two ways. The first is the refusal to migrate back toward proper diversification because one very successful investment would, were it sold, generate substantial capital gains taxation.

In fact, at current rates, nothing generates substantial capital gains taxation *as a percentage of the gain itself.* Paying 15% in taxes to repatriate a great gain is an opportunity which only a pig would turn away from.

A capital gains pig will invariably identify himself to the world by denominating the issue in the number of dollars in taxes he would have to pay if he sold. Thus: "I can't sell my Merck; I'd have to pay a million and a half dollars in taxes." The pig hopes you won't notice—as he has steeled himself single-mindedly not to notice—that he has just announced that *he has a $10 million profit in Merck.* Were he to say, in so many words, "I can't bring myself to pay even a 15% tax in order to take the remaining 85% out of harm's way," even he would hear himself going "Oink."

(I said, toward the beginning of this chapter, that you often see people making a number of the Eight Great Mistakes simultaneously. And you will surely not have failed to notice that euphoria, unconscious speculation and leverage are a common, and invariably fatal, trifecta. In the case of the capital gains pig, the deadly duo will be the Cost-Basis Heuristic leading to underdiversification. Merck will get to be a third of his portfolio, then half, then even more. And one fine day, Merck will announce its Vioxx problem, and the guy who wouldn't pay a 15% tax will see his stock trade down 24% in one day.)

The other major manifestation of the CBH is, of course, "I can't take the loss." Doesn't matter that the fundamentals have completely changed; indeed no objectively verifiable fact matters. The guy paid $30 for the stock (or the fund); it's now $19, *and that has become, in and of itself, his reason for holding it.*

How, finally, do you "convince" someone not to throw himself on one or more of these grenades? Right: you don't, because (a) you can't; (b) it's not your job; and (c) it's beneath your dignity. Advisors who keep wrangling with suicidal "investors" over the same issue become, thereby, crazier than the person they're arguing with. Have the courage and the self-respect to go prospect for somebody sane.

Even that is beside the point of this chapter, which is, of course:

> ON THE PIVOTAL DAYS OF AN ADVISORY RELATIONSHIP, THE ESSENCE OF GOOD BEHAVIORAL ADVICE IS SIMPLY HEADING OFF A LOOMING BAD BEHAVIOR.

SUMMARY

- Learning what to do right—the six steps—is one approach to the management of investor behavior. *Inverting* that lesson—studying what the investor is most likely to want to do wrong, and why—is the other.

- To a tremendous extent, outstanding real-life investment success does not rely on doing anything brilliant, but on simply avoiding The Big Mistake. It's not about hitting the most great shots, but rather the fewest really terrible shots.

- The moments of the BIC's greatest value, therefore, are those in which the client is winding up to make a classic mistake. And all the BIC needs to do is to impress upon the client that *"You must not do that."*

- *Telling* the client not to do something is unfortunately much less than half the battle; *getting* the client not to do it is the rest. This will be a pure function of how strong the relationship is, and how behaviorally prepared the BIC has rendered the client.

- There are Eight Great Mistakes—eight hydra-like heads growing out of the body of The Big Mistake. None is objectively more dangerous than another; indeed, the most dangerous one is that which the client is winding himself up to make right now.

- Some of the Eight Great Mistakes are often made simultaneously; a couple of them are usually made one right after the other.

- **Overdiversification:** buying things without selling other things, which leads to a condition in which the investor, by buying everything, ends up owning nothing. He's not even an investor anymore; he's a collector.

§ **Underdiversification:** the fatal narrowing of a portfolio down to essentially one idea—one deadly certainty, if you will—be it a new era or the end of the world. Another iteration of this Great Mistake is the overconcentrated stock position: loving a stock that will never love you back, in the benighted conviction that love renders you exempt from the iron law of creative destruction. *It does not.*

§ **Euphoria:** often mislabeled "greed," it's the loss of an adult sense of principal risk. In the euphoric state, investors unconsciously define "risk" as "the danger that other people are making more money than I am."

§ **Panic:** invariably follows episodes of euphoria, and is usually as deep as the euphoria was high. It manifests as an unconscious belief that the curve of equity returns has been permanently broken, or at least that equities will not come back in the investor's lifetime. This psychology begets the impulse to capitulate at any price; when most investors are doing this, an epochal market bottom is being formed, at prices which will probably never be seen again.

§ **Leverage:** not leverage as a rational spreading of anticipated costs against anticipated higher returns—which is as sensible as it is exquisitely rare—but leverage as the wrong loan on the wrong terms to do the wrong things at the wrong times for the wrong reasons.

Example: borrowing to buy Amazon.com well north of $200 a share when its CEO was *Time*'s man of the year in December 1999. Everyone who did this either zeroed out, or made good on the loan such that they will be in the hole on this investment for years if not decades.

§ **Speculating when you still think you're investing:** and not seeing that you've gone over to the dark side. Putting money into a miracle—at the prices the venture capitalists extract from public investors rushing to cash in—is very different from investing in a business; this distinction is lost when people cross over. It will help if you remember always that VCs see you as their exit strategy.

Similarly, all synthetic instruments with an ending value of zero after expiration are speculations, as are all hedges. I will leave to your professional judgment whether professionally managed portfolios of such speculations become investments.

This mistake is often made in concert with underdiversification, euphoria and leverage. The combined effect is almost invariably lethal.

§ **Investing for current yield instead of for total return:** the classic retiree's mistake. It ignores the fact that the relationship between current yield and long-term total return is inverse, and that the only rational test of an investment's income potential over time is its total return.

§ **Letting your cost basis dictate your investment decisions:** your cost is no determinant of an investment's value; indeed, yours are sunk costs, and the investment's value today is what someone will pay you for it. Your investments, in other words, do not know what you paid for them, and would not behave any differently if they did. Tune out tax consequences; tune out your ego. Just ask yourself if this investment—in this amount—is a desirable component of a well-diversified portfolio. If it is not, cut back on it until it is, or liquidate it altogether.

§ Expect that, on the pivotal days of the advisor/client relationship, the essence of good advice is no more or less than: ***"You must not do that."***

BOOK THREE

THE BEHAVIORAL CONVERSATION

ADVOCATING FOR THE VALUE
OF BEHAVIOR MANAGEMENT

"WHAT'S YOUR TRACK RECORD?"

How many prospecting interviews have you been involved in—and through how many more will you suffer, until you become a believing, practicing BIC—during which this Mother of All Wrong Questions has frozen your blood and stopped your heart?

For this question manages to encapsulate, in just four little words, the three governing misperceptions that most investors bring to portfolio management, and therefore to any potential advisor/advisee relationship:

1. It assumes that the primary function of a financial advisor is portfolio management. ***But it's not:*** it's financial planning. A portfolio has no rational function other than as the servant of a plan. Thus, the highest and noblest function of an advisor is planning.

2. It assumes that the primary determinant of investment success is portfolio performance. ***But it's not:*** it's investor behavior. So

the second highest, second most noble function of an advisor is as a behavior modifier.

3. It assumes that the advisor is prepared to be judged on the basis of one number, which probably doesn't exist, and wouldn't mean anything even if it did. **But she's not:** she is willing to be judged only on the basis of her ethical standards, her devotion to her clients' best interests, and her professional competence as a planner and a behavioral coach.

"What's your track record" is therefore the very worst question you can be asked, and since there is no possible right answer to it, you must never attempt a direct answer. As in any situation where the prospect tries to set the agenda in the wrong terms, your first duty is to re-set the agenda in your own healthy, planning-oriented, behavior-driven terms. *Nothing good can happen, in this or any other professional conversation, until you take firm control of the agenda.*

How you set the agenda—or, as in this example, regain control of it—is an interesting question, but it can never be the threshold issue, any more than any "how to" issue can be. (Methodology and technique are always, at best, secondary issues.)

Reason from first principles: *the conversation has to begin with (a) your personal statement of the primacy of planning and behavior as the critical determinants of lifetime return, and (b) your corollary statement of the nature and value of your behavioral advice.* Until you are prepared to make those two statements, any colloquy between you and the prospect is just mood-setting.

So, for example, asked the inane question about his track record, the BIC might very gently answer the question with a parrying question:

BIC: *Which one?*

PROSPECT: *Uh, yours. I mean, your track record. You do have a track record, do you not?*

BIC: *I must have about 200 of them, inasmuch as I'm the advisor to about that number of client families and households. So I guess I'm managing upwards of 200 differing portfolios, each geared to the client's personal goals and emotional makeup. That must mean I have something like 200 different "track records," although I'll be blessed if I could tell you what any one of them is. Don't think it matters much...(BIC lapses into companionable silence).*

P: *What on earth are you talking about?*

Dear reader, please note what has just happened here. Without being in the least argumentative, the BIC has just politely refused to answer the question. Instead, he has made a lovely little introductory statement of what he does, which has (quite deliberately) gotten the prospect so confused that he blurted out an open-ended question. Now the BIC can re-set the agenda, and make his statement.

BIC: *I'm essentially a financial planner first, and a portfolio manager only in the sense that my portfolios are the funding media for the plans. A portfolio is simply a tool for the realization of my client's goals; it's never an end in itself.*

  So the first thing I work to determine is what you're trying to accomplish, how much time you've got in which to accomplish it, and what resources you bring to the effort to achieve your goals. Then, together, we develop an investment strategy: a plan for reaching your goals. Then, and only then, I design a portfolio which, at long-term historical rates of return, will get you where you need to go.

  That's the easy part, and it might consume five of the 10,000 days we're going to be working together, assuming I'm your advisor for 30 years.

Then our real work together begins. Once we've created a high quality portfolio of investments that are extremely well-suited to your long-term goals, I become, in a very real sense, your behavioral coach—helping you, over those next 10,000 days (and even longer, let's hope) to continue to make good decisions, and avoid making inappropriate decisions, about what to do—and what not to do—regarding the portfolio.

I don't say that the investments I recommend will "outperform" most of your neighbors' investments.

I certainly don't rule it out; I just can't promise it—nor can any other advisor—and it has almost no connection with what I do for my clients.

I say that, using the principles I practice, you should end up with a far better lifetime return than do most of your neighbors.

Seeing that these are two different things, and why they're two different things, is the beginning of wisdom—and the beginning of an understanding of what I do.

*In concept, that's the way I try to help my clients achieve their financial objectives. As you can see, my approach is goal-focused and planning-driven, rather than being based on some attempt to outguess the economy or the markets. I'm convinced that all successful investing involves constantly **acting** toward the realization of goals, and all unsuccessful investing is based on **reacting** to whatever the markets happen to be doing at the moment.*

The next step, then, would be for us to get a shared understanding of your most important financial goals. Then we would look at your current financial condition—broadly speaking, what you own less what you owe—and consider the time remaining toward the realization of your objec-

*tives: **when** do you want to retire; **when** do the grandchildren you're investing for start college, and so forth.*

Finally, we look at what additional sums you can add to your investments before you need to start drawing an income from them, and what other resources you can rely on. Those calculations will tell you what rates of return you need to achieve, and from there we can practically back into an appropriate portfolio.

I'd like, next, to offer you more specific examples of what I mean by my behavioral coaching, and to tell you what I charge. But first, does the planning approach I've described seem to you an intelligent way for us to begin? Or does it suggest any questions you want to ask me right now?

It should be clear to you that this three-minute statement, or any reasonable approximation of it, will cause market maniacs, performance junkies and similarly disturbed individuals to flip out on the spot, and to de-select themselves. This is in keeping with a critically important BIC dictum, which states that the most effective way to get crazies off The Ark is simply never to let them on in the first place.

You may tell yourself—presented with a potential $5 million account by the third runner-up in the Alfred E. Newman look-alike contest, who is just at the moment frothing at the mouth and babbling something about the Kondratieff wave theory—that once he gets to know you, you'll be able to change him. It is my sad duty to disclose to you two corollary truths: (a) you can't change anybody, if only because (b) people don't change. You ignore these verities at your peril. And don't kid yourself: you'll know in the first 20 minutes of the first conversation who's going to make it and who is not, just from the way they react to the above statement.

You have to stand for something, or you'll stand for anything. In this timing and selection culture, subtlety and/or gradualism about your planning/behavioral approach will prove to be counterproductive: people simply won't hear you. At best they'll be confused, and at worst they'll hear what they expect (and want) to hear: an advisor telling them they'll "outperform" *as they have always defined that term.* It's a formula for stress, heartbreak, and quite possibly arbitration. *Tell people the absolute, unvarnished truth right from the get-go, and let the chips fall where they may.* The time- and energy-saving power of the absolute truth cannot be overstated.

Now, having established the fact that you are a planner first and foremost, and that you create and maintain investment portfolios only pursuant to a plan, you must realize and accept the singular constraint that this places on you and your practice. To wit: *the Behavioral Investment Counselor never accepts the management of a portfolio without a plan.* I say again: *no portfolio without a plan, and—or at the very least—an investment policy statement.* If you accept portfolio management in the absence of a written plan and/or policy statement, you will have signed up to run in a performance derby—a race you are bound to lose—and the tragedy is that, when the "relationship" comes to its inevitably ignominious end, you will have no one to blame but yourself.

If an investment account is not to be measured against a plan, then it can only be measured against "the market," or some benchmark, or the investor's fevered hallucinations about how much money his neighbors are making. And those are the accounts you always lose. (That is, if you're lucky; if you're not, the "client" just keeps hanging around, ritually trying to tear out your liver with chronic complaints about your "underperformance.")

An investment account not rooted in a plan is written on the rain; it will blow this way and that with the mood of the moment, and with whatever chemical imbalance afflicts the "client" after he's watched his 64th straight hour of CNBC. You've absolutely got to have a written document back to which you can take your client, in order to be able to show him, time and again, that some particular thing he wishes to do—always in *reaction* to something the market is doing—will skew, if not destroy, the plan. In extreme moments of speculative euphoria or panic-stricken capitulation, you sitting there mumbling "Don't you remember that we agreed…" just isn't going to cut it.

Now, for purposes of completing the logic of this chapter, we'll assume the prospect asks no particular questions at the end of the three-minute statement above—though the good people will always appreciate your giving them the opportunity to do so. We'll shortly proceed to establish a formula for questions and objections handling; you'll be better served, just at the moment, by seeing the rest of the BIC's opening statement.

BIC: *My philosophy of advice is that by far the most important factor determining the long-term investment returns people get in real life is their own behavior. So, for example, the issue for me isn't predicting when markets will peak or bottom out—which no one can consistently do—but managing the way my clients respond to those periods of euphoria near market tops, and to the panic and despair which are very human reactions around market bottoms.*

So I wouldn't be trying, for instance, to predict when the dot. com bubble would end; I'd be trying to make sure my clients never got overly exposed to dot.com in the first place. Conversely, I wouldn't be trying to pick a point at which a declining market would bottom; I'd be working to make sure my clients did not panic out of a bear market, but instead continued investing at fire-sale prices, thereby getting that much closer to their goals.

These are just a couple of the more obvious examples of the tremendous power of behavioral advice to alter the course of people's lifetime investing outcomes. And I hope they make clear to you the basis for my earlier statement: that I couldn't guarantee that your investments would be "outperforming," at any given moment, most of your peers' investments. But I can feel reasonably sure that you'd be achieving better long-

term results than were most of your peers, simply because I had helped you avoid some of the very common human mistakes that most people are making most of the time.

The way I charge for my advice is twofold. There is a fixed cost for the full financial plan which becomes the basis for the creation and management of the portfolio. (BIC states it, at the very least in ballpark terms.) My only other cost to you is one percent of the investment assets under management. I would invite you, in the strongest possible terms, to see that expense as being purely a function of my behavioral advice.

In other words, assume—as I certainly do—that I'm charging nothing for such portfolio services as allocating your investments among the different asset classes, choosing the investments themselves, monitoring the portfolio, routine service needs you may have from time to time, and a full-scale annual review with you, your professional advisors, and as many members of your family as you can possibly persuade to attend. I hope you will view these services simply as a portfolio of courtesies.

In effect, you have to conclude that my behavioral advice—coaching you to continue to do the right things, and to avoid doing the wrong things, especially when your peers are giving in to the fads or fears of the moment—is worth a great deal more than one percent per year.

You have to look at it, I think, almost as you would an insurance premium. This analogy is far from perfect, but: you pay a small fraction of the value of your home each year to insure against its burning down. And I charge one percent a year to try to keep you, as a friend, from ill-considered decisions which would ultimately cost the portfolio multiples of one percent per year. Any advisor has to offer value in excess of his cost, or it would be irrational to hire him; this is my statement of cost and value.

> *I realize that I've given you a very great deal to think about,*
> *and I appreciate your giving me the time to state the nature of*
> *my value to my clients. That statement is complete now, and I*
> *would very much welcome your comments or questions.*

The preceding statement can easily be delivered within four minutes. Together with the opening statement you read earlier, then, you may infer that *a clear, concise, unambiguous and deeply felt exposition of the Behavioral Investment Counselor's services, costs and ultimate value can almost effortlessly be made in seven minutes.* I can only add that I would be hard pressed to understand why you would need to say more, in this first complete statement of what you propose to do for people, *nor how you could ethically say less.*

Now before any reader commences to have a cow over some or another inconsequential detail of this very general rendering, please note the following two points:

a. The statement says that you charge separately for the plan. Such is my recommendation. My personal experience of financial planning, like that of hundreds of advisors I've counseled over the years, indicates that *a plan which a prospect receives at no cost will be unconsciously assumed by him to have no value.* Or at the very least, since the prospect has neither an emotional nor a financial investment in the plan, he will feel no impetus to put it into action. The converse is also quite wonderfully true: if they paid, say, $3000 for the plan, there's a pretty good chance they're going to implement it, if only because they don't want the three thousand bucks to have gone up the flue.

That's the very human rationale for my recommendation that the plan be charged for; that it oughtn't to be part of the prospecting process. I rather doubt that the entire logic of this chapter, much less of this book, would come crashing down in smithereens if you were not persuaded by this recommendation. Do try not to sweat the small stuff.

b. The statement is premised on a fee of one percent of the invested assets. This was for illustrative purposes only. (Although, in the interest of full disclosure, were I starting back into personal practice tomorrow, this is how I would charge. Such is my belief in the power of behavioral counseling, and in my own ability to dispense it to life-altering effect.)

It is not a statement that asset-based fees are better, worse, more morally right or less morally wrong than any other method of compensation you may elect. If in fact you have chosen some other way to charge, live long and prosper. Take out the reference to fees in the script above, and insert your preferred compensation method. Just make absolutely sure a prospect would understand what you charge, and—even more importantly—that you charge it purely for behavior modification. I have to hurry and finish this paragraph now, as this whole subject puts me almost immediately into deep REM sleep.

(Just before dozing off, need I add that—if your one percent is mushed together with asset management fees and other charges, as is often the case with separately managed accounts—you will wish to identify and refer only to that part of the wrap fee which is your compensation? No? I thought not; too obvious. Sorry to have bothered you. Zzzzzz...)

———

Spend seven minutes right now, reading the BIC's statement all the way through *out loud*, as one complete thought. Indeed, if the means are available, record your reading of it. Then play it back, and assess the extent to which you are—or aren't—convinced by what you hear, as opposed to what you've read.

A while ago in this book, I said that the question you would ultimately have to answer was not whether you understood behavior modification as a value proposition, *but whether you believed it.* I said also that—since there are no charts, graphs or scattergrams with which to "prove" the efficacy of behavioral advice, and since it may strike the prospect as an entirely new concept—*the messenger becomes the message.* I can sum up everything I've learned in four decades about the art of principled persuasion in six words:

WHEN I BELIEVE, I AM BELIEVED.

And, brothers and sisters, be assured of this: that if there is a scintilla of doubt, uncertainty or hesitation coming off you during those seven minutes, you're done for. To be sure, you need to understand the theory and practice of behavioral investment counseling right down to the ground, and I solemnly promise you that, by the time you finish reading this book, you will. *But "understanding" will not get you where you need to go.* As the late Tug McGraw so memorably said, all those years ago: *You gotta believe.*

That being the case, let us review what you should have come to believe up to this point. *Do not worry that you can't yet answer all the myriad questions and objections you know you're going to hear.* We'll get to those issues momentarily. But first, you have to realize that you are, in fact, standing on the moral high ground: that there are powerful answers to all the questions, and that there are no—I repeat, no—valid objections. And that is one intensely liberating realization. *We are primarily telling, not primarily selling.* We're simply reporting incontrovertible—if still countercultural—truth.

A neurosurgeon diagnoses and prescribes; he doesn't try to prove anything. Guy walks into the neurosurgeon's office; says, "I have these increasingly intense headaches. I've been taking non-prescription pain relievers in increasing doses, and getting less and less relief. I'm starting to think there might be something really wrong here." Doc puts him through the usual battery of tests, analyzes his findings, and sits down with the guy a few days later.

Doc says, "I've got some good news and some bad news. The bad news is you've got a brain aneurysm. Looks like you've had it for a while, and that it's fixing to blow. If it blows, you'll be dead before you hit the ground. That concludes the bad news. The good news—and it's very good news indeed—is that the aneurysm is in a very obvious, very reachable place. No operation on the brain is entirely routine, but I've done this one a great many times before, and always successfully. We'll relieve the aneurysm, and you'll have no lasting effects; you'll be good as new.

"Now, I want you to go downstairs, get in a cab—don't drive yourself—and go to the hospital. I'll have them waiting for you, and they'll get you ready. Tomorrow morning, I'll operate, and by nightfall, your family should be able to visit you."

Patient says, "I don't know; I was just wondering if you could give me something prescription strength—stronger than Advil or Aleve—so I could feel better."

Note carefully that the neurosurgeon does not, at that point, try to convince the doomed fish of anything in particular. He does not commence to leap about his office, putting up charts and graphs which show the high mortality rate from burst aneurysms, nor that document his credentials or demonstrate his accomplishments. He does not attempt to present himself as the low-cost neurosurgeon in town, nor does he offer the guy a discount. There is a little button on his desk, and when he presses it, he is connected to his assistant's desk, outside his office. He now presses said button, and intones the magic monosyllable:

"NEXT."

Brothers and sisters, go thou and do likewise. We know that a portfolio without a plan is a rudderless vessel; this is beyond dispute. **We know that timing and selection do not work**; this, too, is beyond dispute, though we may meet many people with really bad headaches who will continue to dispute it. (A guy who panicked out of equities in 2002, and/or in 2008, is going to tell you that behavior can't be the critical variable? And you're going to debate with him? Don't look now, but he's no longer the crazy person in the conversation.)

We know that a goal-focused, planning-driven portfolio—steered by the stars of faith, patience and discipline; properly asset allocated, broadly diversified and regularly rebalanced—is most investors' only hope of achieving superior, long-term, real-life returns. We know, finally, that immutable human nature being what it is, most investors will not be able to maintain the course described in the foregoing sentence without the ministrations of a Behavioral Investment Counselor.

These beliefs will have to be enough…and they surely are. Indeed, everything else is commentary. Yes, this book will get you prepared to answer all the important questions, and to counter all the major objections. But at the same time, let me caution you against trying to convince anyone of anything. It is not your function to convince, any more than it is the neurosurgeon's; indeed, it is as beneath your dignity as it is his. ***You cannot want more financial peace for an investor than he wants for himself. You cannot help anyone who refuses to be helped by you now.***

Read the BIC's statement. Read it, speak it, repeat it, record it. Then begin refining it into your own language and style, until every word, and even every pause, is uniquely your own—that is, until you literally own it.

But do not ever ask anyone to believe it. Ask them to believe you. ***It isn't the same thing.***

SUMMARY

- The most effective way of getting "performance" maniacs off The Ark is simply never to let them on in the first place. Make a clear and unequivocal statement, right from the jump, (a) of the primacy of planning and of behavior as the critical elements of lifetime return and (b) of the nature and value of your behavioral advice. Don't be subtle about this statement, and don't think you can change anybody. You can't.

- Your meeting, your agenda. If the prospect walks in and attempts to set the agenda, your first job is to re-set it, in your own healthy terms.

- You can make a very clear statement of what we do conceptually in about seven minutes. Keep it brief, businesslike, and confident of success. Focus on the countercultural nature of what you're saying, and you'll choke. Focus on the fact that it's the only truly rational approach, and you'll glide.

- Never accept the responsibility for portfolio management without a written plan and/or an investment policy statement. Portfolio management without a plan can't help but degenerate into a performance derby.

- Rehearse, record, repeat. Practice, practice, practice. Refine your seven minutes until they become not merely yours, but you. The messenger is the message. When you believe, you'll be believed, and not until.

- Do not ask people to believe what you're saying. Invite them to believe *you*. These are two entirely different appeals.

9

REFINING THE ART OF
PRINCIPLED PERSUASION

AS YOU COME TO THE END OF YOUR MAGISTERIAL seven-minute statement—and just before you start getting emotionally tangled up in the prospect's immediate responses thereto—take a deep breath, and remind yourself of the single most important truth regarding the conversation you're having. It is this: *the prospect is not interviewing you, as much as you are interviewing him.*

Though you are indeed the neurosurgeon, and the prospect with whom you are sitting indeed has an aneurysm, this analogy may appear to break down at the front end, if in fact *he didn't initiate contact by consulting you; you prospected him.* Until the day you have so many referrals/introductions from existing clients that you have neither the time nor even the need to prospect, assume that prospecting is the mode in which you'll be working. (And be assured that that day is surely coming to the BIC, just as it is never coming to the advisor vainly trying to sell selection and timing.) That's why I recommend that you make every effort to have prospects come to your office for the initial interview, if at all possible.

But no matter where that first conversation takes place, as soon as you've made your seven-minute statement, sit back and evoke a mental image of yourself adjusting your white coat and taking off your stethoscope. This is your meeting; it is your agenda, and you have just stated several life-altering truths.

These truths include, but are not limited to: (a) goals dictate plans, (b) plans dictate asset allocation, (c) asset allocation dictates disciplined diversification into the right *kinds* of investments, (d) from there on, the critical variable is behavior, and you're the behavior modifier. And—oh, yes—(e) timing and selection can't be done scientifically, and that's fine, because they don't matter much.

Now: does the prospect want to have the operation, so that he can live out a rich, full life? Or does he want, however gradually, to drop dead? Those are the questions he has to be led to ask himself, and the process of bringing him to that realization is what I call the art of principled persuasion. If that phrase is new to you, and you don't immediately have a conceptual handle on it, let me clarify: when I came into the profession, a hundred years ago, it was called "selling."

Indeed, I was not trained to be a financial planner—neither the job title nor even the process existed at the time—but rather as a securities salesman. You took a product (or just a stock idea), you pitched it to people as hard as you could, then you answered questions, overcame objections, and kept closing until you got the sale or got thrown out. It was a fairly terrible way to live, but—paradoxically enough—it was wonderful training, and I'll always be inexpressibly glad that I had that training.

If, over time, selling became, for me, principled persuasion—if it went from getting someone to buy a stock to getting him to make the right financial decisions for his family's future security, even when he didn't want to—the core beliefs and the skills remained remarkably constant. Reduced to three ideas, these are:

1. that the plan and the portfolio I propose will be of singular, last-

ing and ultimately decisive value to the prospect and his family, and that that value far exceeds the costs he is asked to bear;

2. that there are, therefore, no valid objections to what I propose, and furthermore that I can overcome all the remaining invalid objections calmly, effortlessly and indeed without conscious thought (because the answers are so obvious and clear); and

3. that I cannot be dismayed or worn down by any number of invalid objections, and will stay calmly in the fight, never giving up, but ending the interview if and when it becomes clear that the prospect has become unalterably opposed to accepting the decisive value I have offered him.

This is my sort of **bushido** code: the way of the warrior. And if I have stressed that you ultimately cannot help someone who actively refuses to be helped, this code is my way of trying to turn him toward the light again and again. It is my method of allowing someone either to run out of objections or—seeing finally that he has run out of them, and still refusing to be helped—in effect to turn his sword on himself.

This is actually quite exhilarating, *irrespective of the outcome*. It does not feel good when the prospect accepts the plan, nor bad when he refuses it. I am unmoved by outcomes, not least because I don't ultimately control them, and it is very unwise to involve yourself emotionally in—much less to judge the quality of your own work by—outcomes you don't control.

The principled persuader, as I have defined her, always feels good, because she is getting her sense of professional self-worth from the quality of the work she is putting out, not whether any particular prospect accepts or rejects the work. The only truly wrong thing she can ever do is to not show her work.

It's axiomatic that an army fighting from the high ground is very difficult to vanquish. The BIC occupies the moral high ground, first of all as the potential author and steward of a family's comprehensive financial plan, and second as the behavioral coach by dint of whose efforts that family will surely get better long-term investment outcomes than they would on their own, or working with a selection-and-timing-oriented advisor.

These are truths of tremendous power. Indeed, you may wish to begin right here to make notes for your own personal statement of belief in your potentialities—a statement you would never make in so many words to prospects, but which forms the core of your own code of belief in yourself.

Note that this has almost nothing to do with experience. If I were a wirehouse trainee who just got registered yesterday, I could immediately access the power of these truths provided only that I were committed to (a) prospect, and never stop prospecting, thereby learning about people as I go, (b) utilize the full resources of my financial planning department, thereby learning about planning as I go, and (c) use pre-packaged portfolios of funds, or other systems of outsourced professional portfolio management—thereby learning about portfolio management (and even about the workings of the capital markets) as I go.

I do not suggest that the financial plan I prepare (or that my colleagues prepare for me) is somehow "the best" plan. I say only that we will work to ensure that it is as closely suited to the client's needs as we can make it, that we will monitor it constantly to keep it that way, and that I personally—as the steward and even the translator of the plan (between the family and the technicians)—will care more about the family's long-term financial success than anyone outside the family. I feel that I cannot be successfully competed with in this latter regard. *No other advisor is going to be more deeply committed to this family's success than I am.*

Nor, as we've already seen so vividly, do I suggest that the portfolios I design (or select) as the funding media for the plan will be "outperforming," at any given moment, most other people's portfolios. I suggest only that, behaviorally counseled, my clients must end up with significantly better long-term, real-life returns than do most other people.

These two beliefs make me unassailable. Another advisor may win the account I seek, almost certainly for the wrong reasons. A prospect may refuse to accept my value proposition, even as the patient with the aneurysm declines to have the operation. Or a prospect may simply not cotton to me personally: the chemistry just isn't there. ***But I can never be beaten, because the great truths I espouse can never not be true.***

The burden of proof is not on me. I can't prove that the sun will come up tomorrow, nor that either my prospect or I will be here to see it if it does. I'm certainly not about to try to prove any financial or investment outcome, much less try to win business with "proof." As I sit before my prospects, I know that a comprehensive plan, a portfolio created and maintained pursuant to the six steps, and my empathetic behavioral counseling are almost certainly their highest-probability path to financial success. My job is simply to give them every opportunity to see that, until they either buy in or bail out.

(Please note that the use of the first person in this chapter, together with the use of the present tense, is not meant to suggest that I'm still running a practice; I am not. I'm using "I" to get you into the habit of thinking in the first person: ***I can do this.*** Still, that may be one important difference between this and some similar books. Not to put too fine a point on it: others can tell you what to do, but I can tell you what I've done.)

And so the conversation continues.

BIC: *This approach to investing—essentially letting the plan dictate the portfolio, and then working to avoid The Big Mistake—is very different from what most advisors still do. And, of course, it's*

> *radically different from all the noise you hear from media about what's hot at the moment, or what crisis is upon us now, and that sort of thing. I can certainly plunge ahead into a discussion of my/our investment process—and I'd love to—but I wonder if there's any question you want to ask right now.*

Again, a good prospect will appreciate that you consult him early and often, rather than trying to overwhelm him with a "pitch." He'll either give you permission to go on, or he'll in fact already have a concern. If it's the latter, I daresay whatever that first question is will tell you an awful lot about him, and about whether this conversation is going anywhere.

PROSPECT: *How do you know when it's the right time to be in or out of the market?*

BIC: *I don't know that, with any consistency, and I'm happy to report that no one else does, either.* (Silence.)

This is a technique I call the non-answer answer. It states an absolute truth, but in a way that is calculated not completely to satisfy the questioner. He will almost be forced to amplify his question, even as the BIC sits there, serenely confident in his answer. Note once again: **The messenger is the message.**

P: *But…isn't that one of the most important things in investing?*

BIC: *It's not, and thank goodness it isn't, because nobody can do it. Read almost any of Warren Buffett's annual reports, and he'll proudly tell you he can't time the market, and never tries.*

   Twenty years ago, the broad market was probably about a quarter of where it is now; 30 years ago, it wasn't a tenth of where it is now. And that's ignoring dividends. For people with your kind of time horizon—10 more years to work and invest, and 30 years after that to try to live on your investments—that's what's really important.

It's not just that you can't time the market; it's that you don't need to.

Consider the difference between this approach, and how it would have sounded if the advisor had blurted out both parts of the answer all at once. He'd have been making an argument, trying to prove something. The non-answer answer causes the prospect to slog deeper into his question, thereby giving the BIC additional information on the misperception behind it. This turns the question into a high, soft lob to the BIC's forehand, and he effortlessly puts it away.

The amateur advisor will take the question at face value, and whip out a chart about the dire consequences of being out of the market on its 40 best days, or some similarly inane statistical/factual demonstration which has never convinced a living soul and never will. Even worse, whenever you use a chart, it becomes the message, and the messenger ceases to be the message, and that's exactly what we ***don't*** want.

Now, back away from the technique issues so that you can look at the important—and even beautiful—conceptual truths upon which the BIC has just gently insisted. They are twofold, and of equal importance. (1) Neither she nor anyone else can time the market, and a long-term investor doesn't need to. (2) She will make no effort to "prove" that you can't time the market, not merely because it is beneath her dignity, but because one can't prove a counterfactual. (Let the prospect try to prove that someone ***can*** time the market, if he cares to.)

We're really, in this scenario, giving the prospect the opportunity to disqualify himself before we spend a lot more time and energy on him. You don't want to go all through the six steps, only to find that the guy is looking for someone who can get him into hot hedge funds. Here's another example.

> P: *How do you know which will be the top-performing funds?*

> BIC: *I don't, and neither does anyone else.* (Silence.)

> BIC: *Excuse me? What about stars, ratings, Forbes's* Honor Roll?

> BIC: *They're all essentially backward looking, because that's all they can be. There's no reliable way of projecting future performance from past performance. Moreover, the nature of the cycle is that sectors and styles that have outperformed in the last several years will often be the underperformers of the next block of time. What I can certainly do is make sure you're in the right **kinds** of funds, given your long-term goals and your ability to handle market volatility. I would urge you to be terribly careful of any advisor who says he can do much more than that.*

I suppose you could romanticize that answer a bit, with blood-curdling examples of managers who shot out the lights, took in huge net inflows, and then went ice cold, but I don't see any substantive difference between that and, say, the 40 best days. That is, I don't hold with trying to demonstrate the obvious, unless the prospect persists. Give any line of questioning a chance to die a natural death; don't try to crush its skull with a tire iron.

Now the thing to do is to try to steer the conversation back to an exposition of your process. You politely gave the prospect, a few pages back, the right to ask a question (indeed, note the use of the singular "question" in the script), but you don't want the interview to lapse into Q&A just yet. You still need to make a number of very clear and compelling statements about what you do and how you do it.

Regardless of whether you use active or passive investments, and regardless of whether you yourself build and maintain the portfolios or farm those functions out to a third party—all of which are equally valid and honorable decisions—*the prospect must immediately get a clear understanding of what your process is… and, equally important, what it is not.*

BIC: *As I've said, the essential driver of the portfolios I oversee is the client's financial plan. It's the plan, rather than any momentary market viewpoint, which dictates the composition of the portfolio. The plan tells you what long-term returns you need, and that, in turn, tells you what asset classes you need to own, and in what mix.*

That decision, which is called asset allocation, becomes the dominant factor in long-term return. That just stands to reason. Over the last eight decades or so, equities have had a compound return around twice that of bonds. After inflation, that margin is closer to three times. So the critical long-term issue has to be the ratio of stocks to bonds in the portfolio—not whether you own growth funds vs. value funds, much less whether you own General Electric vs. Exxon Mobil.

When you have a plan, and an asset allocation appropriate to that plan, you've already made the two key decisions that are going to determine the vast majority of your lifetime return. The next step is getting broadly diversified within those asset classes. We can talk more about diversification when and if we proceed to creating a portfolio for you. But as a general rule, diversification simply means, to me, never owning enough of

> *any one idea to be able to make a killing in it...**nor to get killed by it.** That just seems common-sensical to you, does it not?*

(Just keeping them in the conversation, here, as well as giving them the opportunity to boil over, if they've a mind to. If they're fixing to flip out over some monomaniacal misconception—or even if their last advisor burned them over something or other—better to find out sooner than later.)

> *Now, I haven't got any scientific way of calibrating this. But my experience and my heart tell me that something like 90% of your lifetime return may already be baked in the cake of these three decisions: the plan, the asset allocation dictated by the plan, and broad diversification within the asset classes—no big bets. Selection—exactly which funds/ETFs/whatever to own—is going to be the smallest determinant of your long-term portfolio return. I'm not unmindful of what a countercultural idea that is, and we can talk about it at whatever length you need to. My only defense is that it's the pure, unvarnished truth.*

> *Having selected a properly asset allocated, broadly diversified portfolio of quality investments, we begin the real work of the rest of your investing lifetime: staying on plan, and running the portfolio off the plan rather than off the economic and financial fads or fears of a particular season. Because your goals probably won't change very much, your plan probably won't change much, either. And because of **that**, since the portfolio is plan-driven, it usually won't change much at all.*

> *Which, believe it or not, is itself a source of better returns. It's been demonstrated pretty conclusively that the more often that people change their portfolios, the lower their return. This again just seems like common sense: the more people flail around, in reaction to the*

impulses of the moment, the more probable it is that they're doing the wrong thing at the wrong time for the wrong reasons.

Beyond that, as I've said, the challenges—and my response to them—are fundamentally behavioral. Getting on plan is easy; staying on plan for years and decades is often terribly hard—too hard, in fact, for most investors.

That's my overall approach, and I've talked plenty long enough. Now it's your turn: what would you like to know?

Read the foregoing statement out loud, consulting your watch, and you should find two things: (a) that it cannot take four minutes, and (b) how very, very good it makes you feel.

To the first point: since your part of this initial interview has taken, *in toto*, 11 minutes (seven from the last chapter, plus these four), these conversations needn't take very long at all, and you should be able to schedule a lot of them. In fact, consider telling any prospect that you only need to see him for 15 minutes, in order to give him a very good understanding of what you do and how you do it.

Assure him that, at the end of those 15 minutes, if there's no common understanding, you will cheerfully get up and leave. But that, during those 15 minutes, the prospect will surely see a time-tested, common-sense approach to superior long-term, real-life investment returns **as well as** the realization of his most important financial goals. Somebody who can say no to that has well and truly disqualified himself. *"Next!"*

To the second point: haven't you been running on the selection-and-timing treadmill to oblivion long enough? Aren't you ready to start a new career and a new life telling people the truth about what an advisor can do, and what she can't do? Are you not ready to be liberated and energized by the planning/behavioral paradigm for delivering consistently superior outcomes?

(And if you're just starting out in the profession, and are dismayed and daunted by all you don't know yet know about the analysis of markets and investments, aren't you empowered beyond your wildest dreams to find (a) that you don't have to, and (b) *that it just doesn't matter very much?*)

Thus, the very first rule of principled persuasion becomes: *make the strongest, most economical statement of the planning/behavioral paradigm that you can, backhandedly blowing up as many popular misperceptions as possible in the process.* (You may not be able to kill the illusion of selection and timing in your opening statement, but you can wound it gravely, such that—when it counterattacks during Q&A, which it probably will—you can finish it off without too much additional exertion.)

Now, before reading on, go back to the script in the last chapter, add this one on to it, get out your recording device, and record the total 11-minute opening statement all the way through. Do this three times. You should find, upon playback, that the third reading sounds to you like the most powerful thing you've ever been able to say to a prospective client...and that you're able to say it, with total conviction, in your own true voice.

9
SUMMARY

- Principled persuasion is the art of staying with a prospect, working calmly through questions and even objections about behavioral counseling—secure in the knowledge that none are valid or unanswerable—until he accepts you, or demonstrates conclusively that he does not want your help. This has nothing to do with trying to "convince" him of anything.

- The principled persuader gets her sense of professional self-worth from the quality of her work—the beauty and truth of telling people about planning and behavior management—not from whether a prospect accepts it or not. It's a numbers game, and she is focused on deserving success, which simply means telling this liberating story to enough people.

- The moral high ground from which the BIC fights the good fight is the unassailable conviction that comprehensive planning and behavioral coaching cannot fail to bring a client family to the upper reaches of long-term, real-life returns.

- With enough staff and vendor support, a new advisor can become a BIC immediately by following these principles.

- Never accept the burden of proof. You can't prove anything, including whether the sun is coming up tomorrow, and whether either you or your prospect will be here to see it even if it does. Your job is calmly to hold the moral high ground until the prospect either buys in or bails out.

- Keep your initial response to a question or objection short, in such a way that it almost demands that the prospect/client amplify his stated concern. This communicates confidence, buys time, and may gain you important additional insight into his real problem.

§ No one can predict the market in the short run, and in the long run what it's going to do is obvious. As I write, it is five times higher than it was five bear markets ago (i.e. from the 1987 crash until now). This is all you can say, and all you need to say. It isn't just that you can't time the market; it's that you don't need to.

§ The BIC welcomes the responsibility to put clients in the right *kinds* of funds/portfolios, given the client's goals. She disclaims, on behalf of herself *and all other advisors*, the ability to predict which of those funds will "outperform" its peers, and considers this issue irrelevant.

§ If you believe that 90% of total lifetime return is baked in the cake of planning, asset allocation and diversification, say so, early and often.

§ Make the strongest, most economical statement of the planning/behavioral paradigm as you can, backhandedly blowing up as many popular misconceptions (chiefly about timing and selection) as possible. Then, be at peace. Good prospects will be intrigued (if not yet "convinced"), and the crazies will de-select themselves. "Next!"

10

Q&A/OBJECTIONS HANDLING:
PRINCIPLES AND PRACTICES

LET'S SAY THAT YOU PERSONALLY WANT—JUST TO pick a number off a bus—half a million dollars of annual income before taxes. Let's say further that, for whatever reasons, your personal income is about half the gross revenues of the practice. We now know that the practice has to bring in a million dollars a year. Now, from whence will that million dollars come?

Let's assume your financial planning fees are effectively a wash: that after all your direct and indirect expenses, a plan for which you charge $3000 ends up costing you pretty close to $3000. In the example we've been using, therefore, the whole requisite million dollars would have to come from your one percent fee, expressed as a percentage of assets under management. This implies the need to have a hundred million dollars under management.

But in what increments? You might be serving a hundred households who have an average of a million dollars with you, which actually has the potential to be a fairly elegant practice. Alternatively, you might be serving (or, more accurately, trying and failing to serve) 500 households with an average of $200,000, which would be a lot like getting pecked to death—slowly and in great pain—by 500 ducks. Which of these—or what other permutation of households and assets—will you choose?

For, make no mistake about it, *you will choose*, consciously or unconsciously. You will (or you won't) decide on a *span of control*: the number of households you can effectively serve in the time you are willing to allot to your business. (I've referred to this elsewhere as the number of available staterooms on The Ark.)

This will (or it won't) dictate an average number of dollars each household must bring onto The Ark in order to purchase a stateroom. For example, if you thought you could only offer superb service to 250 households while still enjoying a richly fulfilling personal life, those households would have to bring an average of $400,000 on board.

The only remaining issue is the minimum. Obviously, for every $200,000 account you take on, you will be constrained to find a $600,000 account. This is, in practice, even less fun than it sounds, which is why I've always advocated solving this problem by making your average your minimum. In this example, nobody gets on The Ark with less than $400,000. Since some voyagers will actually bring more, *and no one will bring less*, this discipline will cause you to overshoot your goals by a comfortable margin of error, inasmuch as the error can only be to the upside.

Four hundred thousand dollars is not, in this glorious era, a whole lot of money. (Neither, for that matter, is $800,000. Or a million dollars.) Therefore, if you're prospecting enough, and gently letting people know right from the jump that 400k is "the threshold of my being able to serve the family really well," you should routinely be interviewing plenty of potential stateroom occupants.

And you may find yourself disqualifying large numbers of them. Well and good. The only reason that advisors ever have troublesome accounts is that they accept those accounts, instead of pressing on with their prospecting in the firm belief that The Ark can and will be peopled by investors who get it.

Bear all this in mind as you begin dealing with the multiplicity of questions, and perhaps even objections, that people will have after your countercultural 11-minute opening statement. Cut the prospects a little slack: *they've almost certainly never heard an advisor talk like this before.* And remember that our code calls for us to answer all questions and effectively counter all objections—in the full realization that there are no valid objections—*until the interviewee demonstrates conclusively that he'll never get it, because he doesn't want to.*

PROSPECT: *I guess I don't understand. Like I said, I'm going into a new job, and I'm coming out of my old employer with $972,000 in my 401(k). I just want to roll it over, and have the portfolio keep growing until I retire.*

BIC: *Precisely. I completely understand. What I'm saying is that I have no idea how to manage a portfolio other than as dictated by a plan. This is obviously your retirement money. But I don't yet know how much of your retirement money it is, how long you have until retirement, nor how much you may be able to add to your retirement savings between now and then. Most of all, I don't know how much of an income you'll need the portfolio to throw off when you stop working, such that you can maintain your dignity and independence in retirement. I simply would not know what to recommend until we had figured all that out together. Surely that makes sense to you, doesn't it?*

The ironclad rule is: no portfolio management without a plan, because otherwise you're just getting sucked into a performance derby, which you're ultimately bound to lose. Granted, performance mania will usually present itself more egregiously than in this example ("What's your track record?"), but beware—and resist—any attempt to get you to accept portfolio management that's cut off from a plan. The very best way to get performance maniacs off The Ark is never to let them on to begin with.

P: *I assume I can split the account between you and my other advisor, to see how you do.*

BIC: *Thank you, but I would simply never accept an account on that basis. I would expect to be responsible for the entire portfolio, or none of it. I'd be surprised if the other advisor didn't say the same thing.*

P: *Well, as a matter of fact, he didn't. Seemed tickled pink to get half of a $972,000 account.*

BIC: *I'll certainly take your word for it, but I still don't think it makes any sense for you and your family, and I still wouldn't do it. Look: the way you're going to get the best real-life return is to make a comprehensive plan with one advisor you implicitly trust. Then build a portfolio that carries the plan forward in a coherent and concentrated way.*

With two advisors' portfolios, you're going to get gaps, redundancies, quite possibly fee inefficiencies, and just general cross-purposes. And you're going to end up judging them against each other by whoever's got the higher return over a year or two or three, which is just random.

Pick the one of us whom your head and your heart tell you will be most personally committed to your financial success, and entrust him with the whole assignment. I'll cheerfully live with your decision.

There came a point, during the Second World War in Europe, that the British Field Marshal Bernard Law Montgomery lobbied Winston Churchill to have the command of Allied forces divided between General Dwight Eisenhower and himself. Ike got wind of this, and quietly let his boss, General George Marshall, know that if this plan were put into action, he would resign and go home. He was prepared to bear the terrible burden of the whole war in Europe, or none of it. Predictably, Montgomery's initiative went nowhere.

The ironclad rule here is: never accept part of an investment account. Be like Ike: take responsibility for the whole war or none of it.

(And a corollary rule: never take responsibility for a portfolio you didn't build. From time to time, you may be asked to give ongoing advice regarding a 401(k) account that some other advisory institution is running. Or someone may try to get you to advise them on an annuity that they "can't" cash out of because of the surrender charge. Decline steadfastly to do anything of this kind. The ironclad rules here are twofold. (A) Never take responsibility for a portfolio over which you do not have the authority, *and for whose management you are not being compensated.* (B) *Only cash gets on The Ark.)*

P: *You're competing with Smith Barney, Northwestern Mutual Life, and the trust department of JPMorgan Chase.*

BIC: *Good heavens, **how?***

P: *Beg pardon?*

BIC: ***How** am I competing with them? What's the basis for comparison?*

P: *Well, fees, I guess...how you've performed.*

BIC: *Gee, I wouldn't dream of competing on that basis—even if we **had** lower fees, or higher past performance, or whatever. Which we **might**, I suppose...for all I know...*

P: *Then why should we hire you?*

BIC: *Why should you hire **any** of us in preference to the three others—that's the question I'd ask. Look, you're talking to four great firms—the three you mention and mine. Putting aside the quality of the individual representative involved, which can vary quite a lot, you're not going to get a bad plan or a bad portfolio from any of us.*

But trying to figure out which one is "best" or "cheapest" in some objective way—I don't know how you're gong to do that, and I think you're going to end up making your-self nuts. If you were a member of my family, I'd advise you not to try to do it that way.

P: *Well, then how in the world **should** we choose?*

BIC: *Let me try to answer you with a story. Way back in 1957, when Warren Buffett was just starting out, he was referred to a wealthy family in Omaha named Davis. This would be the first really important client he would have outside his family, and so he went over there, and made his pre-sentation, and left—and the Davises didn't know what to make of him. He was 27, and kind of odd-looking, and the family just kept talking back and forth, but they couldn't decide what to do. And then Mrs. Davis spoke up, and she just said, **"I like everything about that young man."** And that was that. It may not seem very scientific, but that's the way I'd like to get chosen—or not at all.*

Look: my practice is strictly limited to 250 client fami-lies. And those people are my life. My commitment to the clients who choose to work with me is simple: I'm going to care more about you, and be more personally devoted to your financial success, than anyone in the world who doesn't have your last name. If somebody else is cheaper, or somebody else puts up better numbers for a year or two—I don't think that stuff matters very much in the long run.

The right advisor for you is the one you and your family trust the most, and have the most personal faith in. If that's me, fine. And if it's not me, fine. But the very best advice I can give you, from my heart, is: choose your advisor the way the Davises decided to hire Warren Buffett. You'll sleep sounder, you'll live longer—and you'll make better decisions together.

The ironclad rule here is: do not compete on the basis of any "objective" criteria. (In fact, if you're invited to make a proposal, decline to do so.) You never win these kinds of beauty contests, and even if you do, you've won for the wrong reasons. Then, someday, the client will stage another beauty contest, and you'll lose. The whole point of being a trusted BIC is to forge unbreakable relationships based on trust, and you can never do that with numbers.

The other lesson of the foregoing script is that sometimes a great little story sells better than any rational argument and/or battery of numbers. Stories and analogies—rather than formal argumentation—show that you're relaxed, and truly knowledgeable about how a financial relationship is really supposed to work. The story of Buffett's pivotal meeting with Dr. Edwin Davis and his family is one such terrific vignette; it appears, among other places, in Roger Lowenstein's superb if somewhat dated biography *Buffett: The Making of an American Capitalist.*

(Another striking thing about that conversation is that despite the dollars and the prestige the Davises could potentially bring him, Buffett didn't trim in any way on his standards: he wouldn't disclose his portfolio, wouldn't report results but once a year, and would only let the partners add to or withdraw from their accounts on December 31. "As badly as Buffett wanted the Davises' capital," Lowenstein concludes, "he didn't want it on any terms but his." You and I can't be Buffett, but we can be excellent financial advisors, by ***holding fast to our standards.*** And who knows? ***Maybe that's exactly what Mrs. Davis liked about him!)***

NICK MURRAY | BEHAVIORAL INVESTMENT COUNSELING

P: *Our bank says it will manage our portfolio for one half of one percent, which is half what you charge.*

BIC: *That might be a valid comparison, if advice were a commodity.* (Silence.)

P: *Are you saying that it isn't a valid comparison?*

BIC: *Yes, exactly. Advice is the un-commodity; it varies quite wildly in quality, as do advisors themselves...or should I say ourselves. Most advisors will never take the time or care that I will in understanding your goals and needs. And most advisors are continuing to render investment advice based on market prognostication, and trying to guess which funds will outperform—an approach I believe is thoroughly discredited, and which invariably leads to substandard returns.*

The "extra" half of one percent I cost must be returned to you many times over, in the form of improved long-term, real-life outcomes which proceed from my essentially behavioral advice at critical moments. If you're not completely convinced of that, let me advise you, as strongly and sincerely as I can: go with the bank, or whoever else is cheapest.

The ironclad rule here is: do not ever let your advice be commoditized. ***Your price is only an issue to the extent that your value is in question.*** Yet we know that the BIC can always deliver premium real-life outcomes, by modifying behavior much more than by tweaking portfolios, which he virtually never does anyway. Do not blame the prospect if he lapses back into the error that you're primarily managing his portfolio; have the courage to insist that you're primarily managing ***him***.

Some other variations on the fee issue:

P: *I simply can't grasp why we would pay you one percent a year if our portfolio didn't change at all.*

BIC: *That can only be my fault. How did I fail to make clear that I charge for advising you to do nothing only when nothing is the perfect, ideal thing for you to do?*

P: *So you're saying that doing nothing is somehow a positive action, and a direct result of specific advice?*

BIC: *Almost always. Moreover, at critical market junctures, nothing is almost impossible for most people to do. You need a really outstanding advisor—if I do say so myself, and I do—to convince you to do nothing when it really counts.*

P: *Then I admit I'm completely confused. Do you mind expanding on this subject just a bit?*

BIC: *Not at all; that's what I'm here for. You see, when markets are rising spectacularly, people naturally want to concentrate their portfolios in the one or two red hot market sectors that are producing spectacular returns. Inside every tortoise, there's a hare struggling to get out, and I try to prevent that. I say, "You have a beautifully diversified portfolio, ideally suited to your most cherished long-term goals. Don't put your plan at risk chasing a fad. **Do nothing.**" And of course, sooner than later, nothing turns out to be the one right thing to have done.*

P: *Yes, in that sense, I suppose I see your point…*

BIC: *The same is true, and perhaps even more so, in the late stages of bear markets. I had any number of clients, in the fall of 2002, who wanted to get completely out of equities and into money market funds. I said—I know you've heard this before, but bear with me—"You have a beauti-*

> *fully diversified portfolio, ideally suited to your most cherished long-term goals. The sky is not falling. This time is never different.* **Do nothing.***"*

P: *Very well; I quite take your point.*

BIC: *No, wait, please: just work this through with me for one more moment, not as an abstraction but in actual percentages. I was able to keep people from panicking out down around S&P 800. Today, at 1200 (or whatever), they're up 50% (or whatever). Do you see that?*

P: *Of course.*

BIC: *Now suppose, from that day to this, I've never changed their portfolios. And I've cheerfully charged them one percent in every one of those seven years (2002 through 2008). How do you think they feel?*

P: *I suppose, if they have any brains, that they feel they spent something like seven percent to make something like 50% (or whatever).*

BIC: *I'm delighted to confirm that that's **exactly** how they feel.*

P: *Wonderful. Now, if I throw my rifle out of my foxhole, and come out with my hands on my head, will you promise to stop shooting at me?*

BIC: *Why, here I thought we were having a perfectly collegial discussion of my fee…*

The ironclad rule here is: don't explain your fee; don't defend your fee; instead, advocate exuberantly for your fee as the absurdly small fraction of your value that it so obviously is *by **demonstrating the decisive value of behavioral advice at critical market turning points.***

Of course, your ability credibly to mount this advocacy is premised on your actually having given this great advice at euphoric tops (like 1999) and panic bottoms (like 2002). This doesn't require that you knew they were tops and bottoms—we've agreed that neither you nor anyone else can consistently know that. It requires only that you had, in those difficult days, the moral courage as well as the long-term business sense to keep saying, "***Stand by your plan.***"

Another variation on the fee issue:

P: *Your fee is $15,000 a year.*

BIC: *My fee is one percent of the account value, and your account is a million and a half dollars. So yes, I suppose it is $15,000. As the value of the account rises, so will the fee; that's my incentive. If the value of the account falls— or I should say when it falls, in a perfectly normal bear market—the fee will fall commensurately, which is what I call walking my talk.*

P: *No, what I mean is…$15,000 is an awful lot of money. It's another cruise that we could take…*

BIC: *Oh, I see what you're doing: you're focusing on the dollar amount of the fee rather than on the percentage of the assets. Even more critical, you're thinking of those dollars as a net cost to you, when in fact they are the purchase price of a much larger net benefit.* (Silence.)

P: *I'm just not following you.*

BIC: *Then let me expand on my answer—but give me leave, please, to discuss the fee as I think it ought to be discussed: as the percentage of the assets it is, and not the random number of dollars.*

       The premise of my cost to you—indeed, I think, any pro-

fessional's cost, including your lawyer, accountant and even doctor—is that our work must be worth much more to you than that cost. You have to believe that my one percent fee buys a pure net benefit, and is never a net cost. That, and not the number of dollars involved, is the critical variable.

To cite just one pertinent example, **[BIC takes the prospect through the 2002 story in the answer above].**

The moral high ground of the BIC's cost—be it fee-based, fee-only, retainer or whatever—is that it cannot fail to be a small fraction of the value she delivers. By continuing to insist on that most fundamental value proposition, the BIC will qualify prospects for the right reason, and disqualify them appropriately, as well. You will just never make a good, appreciative client out of someone who carps about your cost, nor will you ever get a quality referral/introduction from him.

Of necessity, this will render you a far better advisor than a lot of your prospects deserve. Thus, you will have to watch a lot of them walk out the door, and in fact will have to send many of them out the door. See them out with a song in your heart: someone better, and with even more capital in need of world-class stewardship, awaits you.

Whenever you turn aside (or are turned aside by) business that is beneath your standards, you make an equivalent deposit of good business in a great cosmic bank. And there it sits, awaiting your claim. Indeed, Ralph Waldo Emerson, in his essay "Compensation," takes the position that your deposit does a lot more than just sit there: "Compound interest on compound interest," says the Sage of Concord, "is the rate and usage of this exchequer."

All you need do is to continue prospecting—looking for that deposit which is surely there, with your name on it. The only way you can fail to find it is to stop looking for it. And the pride you experience from not compromising your principles should supply you with more than enough fuel to keep looking.

10

SUMMARY

⤚

๑ Common questions and objections will almost always be rooted in common misperceptions, due to the countercultural nature of what you're proposing. Realizing this, you will strive not so much to answer (much less "overcome") them, but rather to clarify the misperception at hand.

๑ Once again: no portfolio without a plan.

๑ Do not split the portfolio management of an account. In addition to gaps, redundancies and fee inefficiencies, it will, by the end of the first 90 days, have degenerated into a performance derby. Be like Ike: accept the whole responsibility, or none.

๑ Never accept responsibility for a portfolio you're not managing and for which you aren't being compensated. Never accept the delivery of securities; only cash gets on The Ark. Start over from scratch, or not at all.

๑ Do not "compete" on any basis but the promise to care more deeply about the client family's success than will any other advisor—indeed, more than anyone without their last name.

๑ Your price is only an issue to the extent that your value is in question. Great financial advice is the un-commodity.

๑ You charge your fee, retainer or whatever even when the portfolio doesn't change all year *because not changing the portfolio was the one superbly right thing for the client to do,* **and because he never could have done it without you.** Indeed, there are years—1999 was one, 2002 another—where "Do nothing; stand by your plan and its beautifully diversified portfolio"—

turned out to be life-forwarding, lifestyle-changing advice, for which you couldn't charge enough even if you didn't effect another portfolio change for ten more years.

§ Never allow your percentage fee (if such is your compensation method) to be discussed in dollars. It is a percentage of the portfolio, and its value is many multiples of that percentage.

§ Whenever you make a courageous, passionate exposition of your potential value, and are turned away, the sum of that account goes into a great cosmic bank, with your name on it. Another prospect is waiting to award you an account that size, and larger. You just have to know this, and to keep prospecting for that account. Nothing and nobody but yourself can keep you from the business you so richly deserve. This is all but a physical principle of nature.

11

Q&A/OBJECTIONS HANDLING:
TIMING AND SELECTION

IN THE LAST CHAPTER, WE FOCUSED ON QUESTIONS about, and potential objections to, your overall process: first planning, then asset allocation, then diversification, then selection (of active or passive portfolios, or both) and then, forever after, behavior management.

The reason for examining only that class of questions/objections was simple: *process, rather than portfolio, is virtually all you would have talked about so far*. Note that in the eleven-odd minutes you've spoken up until now, all you've said about the portfolio is (a) that it would be ideally suited to carrying forward the goals of the plan, (b) that it would be beautifully diversified, and (c) that, once in place, it probably wouldn't change very much.

Portfolio construction is beyond (or ought I to say beneath) the scope of this book, for two reasons, both of which should be pretty obvious to you by now. (1) In the great scheme of things, it simply cannot matter very much. (2) I personally find the whole subject intolerably boring. I said everything I'm going to say about it in

Chapter 6, and frankly had trouble staying awake even then.

The BIC cannot imagine that portfolio composition can govern even ten percent of long-term, real-life return. (My personal guess is that it's much less.) She reasons as follows: first, having a comprehensive financial plan, and running a portfolio off that plan rather than off a view of the markets, must be a huge positive element of overall return.

Asset allocation dictated by the plan, which will in most cases probably be overwhelmingly in equities, must be the critical determinant of *portfolio* return, *viz.* Brinson. Disciplined diversification within the equity asset class—capturing the full ride of equities with something less, at any given moment, than the full volatility— must be another significant contributor. So, to a lesser extent, must rebalancing. *Thereafter, year in and year out, behavior modification must loom over everything as the dominant determinant of real-life total return.*

In that great tapestry of return—over the investing lifetime of a family—what difference will it make how you weighted growth vs. value, or whether you did or didn't hedge the foreign currency exposure in your emerging markets funds, or which small-cap value manager you hired? Can it be even as much as ten percent?

Where you come down on these issues will obviously dictate both the nature of your conversation with prospective clients, and the spirit in which you respond to market- and portfolio-oriented questions and objections.

I will leave to your discretion a scripting of your portfolio design/ management approach, for the simple reason that I leave that approach itself to you. In the context of presenting, and if need be defending, that approach, I simply offer the following suggestion. *Keep it very short, and very light.* The first interview should focus on process and planning. There can logically be no detailed discussion of a portfolio until a plan has taken shape. Make a brief, general statement of your portfolio management philosophy, if for no other reason than to smoke out and disqualify someone who is bound to take violent exception to that philosophy. *That statement cannot possibly be more than three to five minutes in length; the shorter the better.*

> *"I build portfolios from a stable of 10 or a dozen managers whom I personally know, and with whom I've been working for an average of X years. I selected them, over time, for their character and relative consistency, not because any of them is shooting the lights out at any given moment. In that sense, I guess I'm a tortoise wrangler, not a hare handicapper. I found out years ago that there's no percentage in handicapping hares, because the hare always loses."*

No one ever loved rhapsodizing about their favorite managers more than I did. In fact, upwards of 20 years ago, I wrote a whole book about how to do it, called **Serious Money**. But that day—or rather that emphasis—has passed, and rightly so.

If you're making an opening statement that's 11 minutes long—heck, call it 15—and you're then going to talk for more than five minutes about portfolio management, you're sending the ultimate mixed message. Here you are, insisting that portfolio selection cannot be ten percent of the real-life outcome, and then you turn right around and talk about portfolios more than a third as much as you spoke about process. At best the prospect is totally confused. At worst he thinks all the palaver about process was an act, and who could blame him?

You can certainly offer a somewhat longer, somewhat more detailed discussion of the composition of the specific portfolio when you present it *in the context of the finished plan*. But even then, it should be done almost as a courtesy: outlining the portfolio as opposed to not outlining it, but certainly not "selling" it. *When the portfolio, even for a moment, becomes the central focus of a plan presentation, all is almost certainly lost.*

Look: virtually every BIC (including me) is a recovering performance junkie, except for the few reading this book who are just entering the profession and haven't had time to get hooked. And the thing about addiction is that you're never cured; you're in remission, but you can always keep that remission going for another day by eschewing the drugs of selection and timing.

And that's especially important when you consider that almost every prospect you meet will also be an addict, even if he appears to be fairly functional, and even if he's not aware of his disease. It's the culture: he gets up every day and turns on CNBC ("How to play this market now!"). He faithfully reads *Money* magazine ("Six hot funds to buy now!"). And he has no idea that every day he's ingesting an addictive poison which in time will kill any chance he has for long-term financial peace. He's so sick, he doesn't just think timing and selection matter, *he thinks they matter more than anything else!*

Consider just two classic lines of prospect inquiry, one focusing on timing and the other on selection.

> PROSPECT: *Is this a good time to get into the market, or should I be waiting for the correction?*

> BIC: *For anyone with your time horizon—seven years to retirement, followed by three decades of trying to live off your investments—there is no wrong time to invest in equities.*

> P: *There sure is if I invest all my money today, and the market goes down 25%.*

> BIC: *There are a couple of ways to think about that, once you set aside trying to predict the market, which neither I nor anyone else can consistently do.*

> *One is to ask: historically, what are the odds, on any given day, of the market being just about to*

go down, say, 25%? Just for fun, do you have any sense of what those odds are?

P: *Odds? I didn't even know there were odds. The guys on CNBC never talk about "odds."*

BIC: *That's about par for the course, in my view. The people on CNBC very rarely talk about anything that matters. Anyway, there've been 13 bear markets, averaging a decline upwards of 30%, since the end of WWII, and they've averaged a bit more than a year from top to bottom. In big round numbers, that's about one year in five.*

Which tells me that, at any given moment, the historical odds against a decline of that magnitude are about four to one. And even that doesn't—or shouldn't—matter to someone with a 30 to 40 year time horizon.

*Because the issue isn't what happens on the relatively infrequent occasions when prices go down that much. What's important is what they do afterward. One week in 1987—from a Wednesday through the following Monday—prices went down nearly 30% in just four trading days. Today's prices are nearly five times higher than they were **the night before that decline started**. And that's not counting compounded dividends.*

There's nobody on the face of the earth who doesn't wish he'd invested every dollar he had the day before that decline. And if you're looking for something to be concerned about, I'd strongly advise you to start right there.

The citizens of the timing and selection culture—worried not so much about losing money as they are about looking stupid—always obsess about being wrong in the near term. Almost all the BIC needs to do, in this regard, is to **help them get obsessed with being wrong in the long term: the tragedy of missing the big, long up move for** *fear of catching the (relatively) small, short down move.*

Now, here's a classic selection question.

> P: *How many stars do these funds you're recommending have?*

> BIC: *I don't really know. Easy enough to look up, I guess, but it won't tell you anything about future performance. And it's perfectly irrelevant to the outcome of your financial plan. (Silence.)*

> P: *Are you actually saying that stars don't matter?*

> BIC: *I'm saying two things. First, since there's no statistical evidence for the persistence of performance, stars—being, like all ratings systems, essentially backward looking—can't predict future relative performance. And second, fund selection has very little to do with the success or failure of your financial plan. Your choice of a small-cap value manager will not determine whether or not you run out of money in retirement.*

> P: *No financial advisor has ever said either of those things to me.*

> BIC: *I implicitly believe that. (Silence.)*

> P: *No, I guess what I meant was: don't superior managers continue to be superior managers?*

> BIC: *Over very long periods of time, they tend to. Two caveats, though. First, you have to be able to tell who's a genuinely superior manager and who's just been riding the trends of the last five years. Second, even the very best managers go through astonishingly long periods where they can't get arrested.*

*There was a wonderful study done in 2007 of all the top-quartile large cap managers for the 10 years through 2006. It found that **92% of those top managers had one three-year rolling period (during those 10 years) in which they were in the bottom half of their peers. And—get this—58% of those top managers spent at least a three year rolling period** in the bottom quartile!*

*The classic example of this phenomenon was a guy who ran off 15 straight years of outperforming the S&P 500— something that's never been done before or since. He then proceeded to put up three years in a row where he was down an average of 10% a year in a market that was essentially flat. And the most consistently successful equity fund of all time ended up with—you guessed it—**one star!***

I'm sorry: I wish there were some scientific way to pick superior managers going forward. But, as you can see, it's a quagmire. I'm very comfortable with my essentially character-driven method of picking reliable people. I hope you'll get comfortable with it, too. But at the end of the day, manager selection is just never going to be critical to the success of your plan. I really don't know what else I can tell you.

Let me be quick to confirm your impression that there's no magic formula to these answers: nothing dazzlingly inventive or brilliantly convincing—other than to the extent that perspective and the unvarnished truth are intrinsically convincing. To a good prospect, they are. And to a bad prospect, they're not. Simple as that.

I'm a neurosurgeon. You have an aneurysm. Without the surgery, you'll drop dead. I can't guarantee that you'll survive the surgery, but I can pretty much assure you that if you don't have it, you'll be dead in a year, before you hit the ground. That's it. What else do you want me to do or say? I don't do bird calls; I don't do knock-knock jokes. I don't discount my fee. ***It is what it is.***

The other-directed amateur advisor, who thinks it's his job to convince people of something, always comes off tense and anxious. As how could he not: he's vested his sense of self-worth, however momentarily, in another person's reaction to what he's saying. But he has no control over that reaction. Heck, that'd make me tense and anxious, too. And about a hundred years ago, it did.

But then, as all BICs must, I became—however slowly and painfully—inner-directed. I decided to tell the pure, unvarnished truth all the time, for three essential reasons. (1) It's the only morally unambiguous way to run my business. (2) It most reliably attracts good prospects and repels bad ones. (3) It creates a situation in which there can be no valid objection to anything I propose. Thus, the pure truth—supported, sparingly, by a well-chosen anecdote/statistic—*becomes my theory of questions-and-objections handling.*

Watch closely:

P: *We compared your portfolio to the one recommended by another advisor, and his outperformed yours over the last five years.*

BIC: *I have no doubt that it did. Now, just for a lark, give me the portfolio he recommended, and tomorrow I'll e-mail you another portfolio that beat his over the last five years. This exercise will have some entertainment value, in that it will demonstrate that anybody can make up a portfolio that beat any other portfolio over the last five years.*

*But—and this is the critical point—you will then be looking at three portfolios, **and you will have no earthly idea which one will beat the other two over the next five years.** Neither will I, and neither will the other advisor. But that will be OK, because it doesn't matter.*

P: *Wait…what? What are you saying?*

BIC: *About which part: make-believe portfolios, no one knowing which will outperform over the next five years, or it not mattering?*

P: *I...we...the other guy said...*

BIC: *Maybe we should just go back to where we were before this other person's portfolio came into the picture.*

First, I'm a financial planner, and I design portfolios that have a high historical probability of achieving the goals of the plan, not portfolios that are intended to beat everybody else's portfolios. That was the basis of the recommendations I made to you.

*Second, there is no statistical evidence for the persistence of performance. That's a fancy way of saying: I can't demonstrate that my portfolio will outperform his over the next five years, **and he can't demonstrate that his will outperform mine**. All he can do—and what he seems to be trying to do—is to convince you that past performance is reliably repeatable, which is, not to put too fine a point on it, a lie.*

*If you want to have some real fun, go back and ask him not what he's recommending today—which is just whatever's been hot for the last five years—but what he and his firm were recommending **five years ago**. You'll find either that he has no answer, or that it was an entirely different list of funds—the **previous** five years' winners. It's a very shabby way to render investment advice, but it's what an awful lot of advisors are still doing.*

Finally, let me repeat that portfolio selection cannot—I'm convinced—account for more than about ten percent of your total lifetime return. The key elements are: making a plan and staying on that plan; asset allocation that would historically get you where you need to go; disciplined diversification within the asset class (or classes), regular rebalancing—and above all, the year-in, year-out behavioral coaching that is my ultimate value.

Taken together, those elements make up the dog. Portfolio selection is the tail. Try not to let the tail wag the dog. That's my story, and I'm sticking to it.

You've just seen, in vivid detail, a practical application of the great truth that there's no valid objection to the BIC's program. Holding the moral high ground of performance—to wit, that there is no statistical evidence for its persistence—is not merely a way of excusing the randomness of your portfolio: ***it is a 100% effective way of freezing the "competition."***

As I suggested earlier: I have no basis to claim that my portfolio recommendations will outperform those of most other advisors, ***and I will very much appreciate being accorded the same courtesy by all the other advisors in the world***. For such is the competitive power of the great truth that there is no statistical evidence for the persistence of performance.

Note, too, from this example, that just because I am a repository and a beacon of transcendent truth, that doesn't mean that if a competitor fights dirty with me, I won't beat him to the ground and then kick him in the head until he is dead. I will, but only if he starts it. Did you see the paragraph about going back and asking him what they were recommending five years ago? That's what he gets. Fair warning to all who would try to compete with a BIC using the lie of performance: do not bring a knife to a gunfight, and do not start a fight you can't finish.

Here's another common issue, which appears to be about timing, but which is really a challenge to the advisor's belief in the merit of her own advice.

P: *You're recommending that we invest the entirety of our legacy from Aunt Sylvia by nightfall, but your firm's chief market strategist, in his weekly comments on your website, says he still sees meaningful risks to the economy and the market. How do you defend your recommendation?*

BIC: *Excuse me, but I have nothing to defend. I'm always happy to explain, to the best of my ability, but I never do or say anything that requires defending, and I certainly haven't in this instance.*

P: *Yes, it was a poor choice of words. But the fact is troubling.*

BIC: *Only if you read something into the facts that isn't really there. You see, the critical issues are twofold. First, our chief market strategist doesn't know you or your goals, and I do. Second, and equally important, he's expressing a short- to intermediate-term market opinion (which will either turn out to be right or wrong), while I'm expressing a strategic imperative based specifically on your goals, which historically is always right.*

       I'm not trying to be right about the market, which I've found that no one can consistently be. I'm trying to position you in the way that offers you the best historical probability of reaching your goals, over the seven remaining years of your working life, and the 30 years (if not more) of your retired life. You need to own equities, and equities have positive returns about 75% to 80% of the time.

       The great risk to you, therefore, is not that you'll be in the next 10% to 20% decline; it's that you'll be out of the next 100% to 200% advance. That decline may be coming, and it may not. But that advance, if history is any guide, must come in time, and I must do everything in my power, as your advisor, to see that you're in it.

*So with all due respect to (whoever rendered the negative opinion), mine is almost certainly the more appropriate counsel **for you.***

You'll have noted a couple of things, I trust, about this colloquy. First, invited to "defend" herself and her recommendation, the BIC politely but very firmly declined. If you are ever to be valued by prospects, you must first value yourself. Just because you are seeking business, you are never to be spoken to disrespectfully.

I recently had an inquiry from one of my newsletter subscribers, detailing his conversations with a prospect who was referred by someone very close to the advisor as well as to the referral. As part of a package of retirement strategies, the advisor recommended a variable annuity. The prospect was clearly suspicious of this, and asked a great many questions, among which was, "Are there any hidden charges?"

The advisor plowed on with his inquiry to me, apparently not registering the fact that his professional ethics had been rather seriously impugned, and that he had inexplicably let this pass. In asking if there were "hidden charges," the prospect had clearly stated that she believed it possible that the advisor had deliberately kept a material fact from her, in order to sell her something. That's the antithesis of trust, and trust is the oxygen of advisory relationships: nothing can live without it. I told the advisor that nothing good could come of continuing the conversation, and nothing did.

Wear your professional ethic like the badge of honor that it is, and let no one sully it. When you let even the slightest disparagement pass, you confirm that you're a person of no consequence, and not to be taken seriously. Guard your sense of self-worth with your life, even—and especially—when you're prospecting.

The other, probably more obvious of the two messages in the conversation above is: don't ever be drawn into a proxy debate with some absent guru whose opinion may be contrary to yours. This will be a virtual constant in your career, particularly in falling markets. A client will press on you the latest screed from the high-profile catastrophist *du jour,* demanding that you opine upon—or, even worse, rebut—it.

First of all, since you proudly operate without a market viewpoint—it's irrelevant to what you do, and the market can't be timed—there is no point in your reading market commentary, be it bearish or even bullish. Much more important, **you understand, and care deeply about, the prospect and his dreams and goals**. The guru neither knows nor cares about him.

———

I leave this discussion with a summary point which should go without saying, but doesn't. And the way I know it doesn't is that I'm always getting subscriber inquiries that bottom-line to: I gave the prospect my most deeply felt advice two months ago; he didn't take it; now I want to go back and try him again; what can I say that's new or different?

I'm simply appalled by this. The general principle is: **once your advice has been turned away, never initiate a conversation with that person—be he prospect or client—ever again.** Whenever you feel tempted to contact him with the same advice, know that you are demeaning yourself, and have the discipline to make a prospecting approach to someone else. If the sick impulse returns, just keep prospecting other people.

This is purely an issue of your own self-respect, which on some days is all you've got. Treasure and honor it. Because if you let it slip away in small, shameful moments of weakness, you may never get it back.

11

SUMMARY

- If portfolio composition can account for no more than about ten percent of lifetime return, you have no business talking about it for more than about ten percent of your initial prospect interview(s). At best the prospect will get confused; at worst, he'll forget all about process—just as you seem to have—and you'll be sucked down into yet another bottomless quagmire of selection "issues."

- You can talk a little more about portfolio composition in the context of presenting the finished plan. But only a little more. Beware sending the ultimate mixed signal.

- For the long-term investor, there is no bad time to get into the market. And in a market that rises 75%–80% of the time, the only right time is now. It is always possible that the market will decline significantly from any given entry point; *it is never probable.*

- Realize—and empathize with—the fact that people aren't so worried about entering the market and losing money. They're worried about entering the market and looking stupid. Don't "overcome the objection." And above all do not tell them the market's going up. *Give them permission to focus on their real time horizons, which is a way of giving them permission to stop worrying about what the market will do next.*

- The risk isn't being in the next 20% downtick; it's being out of the next 100% uptick.

- Never quote stars, and if asked, assert that you do not know. Work to make that answer true.

- The best managers in the world go through multi-year sojourns in the doghouse. The last three to five years' performance at best tells you nothing, and at worst is a perverse indicator.

- Show me any portfolio that's outperformed my recommended portfolio over the last five years, and by nightfall I'll send you a portfolio that outperformed both. (Anybody can make up a portfolio that beat any other portfolio in some past period, just by underdiversifying into the recently hottest sectors and/or taking on more uncompensated risk.) The point is that no one will know which of the three will beat the other two going forward.

  Also, invite your prospects to ask the "competitor" what he was recommending five years ago; it will turn out to be all different funds/managers. Normally, the BIC is content to freeze the "competition" over the unpredictability of future relative performance. But fight dirty with him on this issue, and he'll kill you.

- Do not read nor comment on the work of an extremist guru, be he bull or—much more probably—bear. It is an attempt by the client to draw you into a debate about the market's direction, and this you must never do. If their goals haven't changed, the portfolio shouldn't change. And a long-term financial planner should never have a market outlook.

- Do not ever let your professional ethics be impugned.

- Once your best, most thoughtful, most carefully-reasoned advice has been turned aside, never initiate contact with that person again. If he calls you, that may be another matter (and it may not). But have some professional pride: do not initiate an offer of advice once your best advice has been rejected.

BOOK FOUR

BEHAVIORAL COUNSEL IN SEASONS OF CRISIS

—

12

BEAR MARKETS:

AN APPRECIATION

AN OLD ZEN PARABLE TELLS OF TWO MONKS, SITTING
in the courtyard of their monastery, observing a flapping pennant.
"The wind is not moving," opined the one monk; "it is the pennant
that is moving." "No," said the other, "the pennant is not moving;
the wind is moving." The oldest and wisest Zen master of them all,
happening by, heard this colloquy, and said, "The wind is not moving. The pennant is not moving. *Your minds are moving*."

This becomes the text for my sermon about bear markets.

Even more than euphoric, "new era" episodes in the equity market
cycle—when people woefully underestimate the risk to their capital—the most dangerous seasons of an investing lifetime are significant, generalized declines in prices, which we call "bear markets." Perversely, at such times, people tend to perceive far more
long-term risk to their capital than is ever really there.

Thus, bear markets are the true testing times for the client, for the
advisor, and most of all for their relationship with each other. How

successful you are at sustaining your clients' faith, patience and discipline when those qualities are under savage, relentless assault will determine, to a very great extent, both the clients' lifetime return and the trajectory of your advisory career.

Bear markets themselves, ironically, are no danger to the long-term investor, because they are so transitory, and because, when the permanent uptrend reasserts itself—four years in five, historically—the subsequent gains eventually dwarf the temporary declines. It is therefore not bear markets which do people in. *The issues are: how surprised are people by a perfectly normal bear market, and what exactly do they think is going on?*

If people have just finished drinking the Kool-Aid of a "new era"— if, as at the turn of this century, they had come to believe that the business cycle and/or the market cycle had been repealed—then they will be *very* surprised, very disappointed, and therefore very pre-disposed to panic and capitulation. Likewise, if people think that the current bear market is different from all the others—that it represents a potentially permanent destruction even of well-diversified, high-quality equity portfolios—they will liquidate their holdings at panic prices which may never be seen again.

And so we observe, yet again, that people's real problem is never what's going on in the markets; *it's what's going on in their minds*. As the Zen master said, "*Their minds are moving.*" This is simply the best news a fledgling BIC could possibly get.

Because it means she doesn't have to fear a bear market, nor try to anticipate it, nor redeploy her clients' assets radically when one strikes, or simply threatens to strike. All she has to do is to guide them through the proper emotional responses—to control the direction in which their minds are moving—until, as they all do, the bear market ends.

This chapter and the next, then, are devoted to three key ideas: (1) understanding the history, the internal logic, and the function of bear markets; (2) preparing clients for bear markets, and then responding appropriately to their fears as a bear market worsens, in such a way as to suppress their proclivity to panic; (3) preparing yourself and your practice, as well as your clients, to greet bear markets as an opportunist rather than as a victim.

First, the technical definition: **a bear market is a period of time during which common stocks are returned to their rightful owners.** That is, stocks that were bid away from good investors by bad investors during euphoric times are, during major market declines, sold back by the flapper to the wise and deserving investor at fire-sale prices. Indeed, scribbled on the back of a postcard, that's not a bad description of the entire market cycle.

And it underlines a great behavioral truth: the wise investor surges enthusiastically forward to take advantage of falling prices (and therefore rising values), even as the flapper flees from them in terror. The former perceives a bear market as a big sale on the great companies in America and the world; the latter perceives it as the long-awaited onset of Armageddon. Note that they are processing exactly the same bear market experience, but that they are reacting to it in opposite ways. What can explain this? Of course: *Their minds are moving.*

There are four essential things you need to know about bear markets, and you have to know them not just intellectually but emotionally, and perhaps even spiritually. (Remember: it is faith in the future rather than knowledge of the future which is the first and greatest of the six steps.)

1. THEY ARE AN ESSENTIAL, ORGANIC ELEMENT IN A NEVER-ENDING CYCLE. As long as human economic actions are dictated by immutable human nature, economies will first overshoot, and then undershoot, their long-term trendlines. In expansionary times, people will borrow too much money to finance marginal enterprises based on overly optimistic projections, and banks will lend it to them. Equity investors will pay premium

prices for unsound IPOs. As a result, the economy will, for some little while, grow beyond its sustainable capacity. Stock prices, which cannot long do anything other than what the economy is doing, will follow suit.

When the reckoning comes—when ill-considered expansions fail, when loans default, when marginally-financed companies go bust, when lenders, consumers and investors pull back too far in revulsion and fear, when an Enron or a Fannie/Freddie suggest that nothing is safe anymore—the economy will sink below its long-term trendline, and pull equity prices down with it. It was—and will be—ever thus. It's human nature. Either embrace it, or realize that you can never be an equity investor.

2. THEY ARE AS COMMON AS DIRT. There have been, as we shall shortly see, 13 bear markets (peak-to-trough declines of about 20% minimum on a closing basis) since the end of the Second World War—which, for better or worse, is my proxy for modernity. Thirteen bear markets in 63 years is an average of one every five years. If you work and accumulate capital for 40 years, on average you're going to go through eight of them, and if you and/or your spouse live 30 years in retirement, you'll get to enjoy six more. Common as dirt. Get used to them.

3. THEY ARE TEMPORARY INTERRUPTIONS OF A PERMANENT UPTREND. Again, as you'll soon observe: the first of the 13 post-WWII bear markets began in May 1946. The S&P index topped out at 19.3. As I write, in the autumn of the thirteenth, it is 1200. Each and every one of those 13 bear markets happened because of significant and often terrifying economic and/or financial crises, and each was faithfully reported in the media as the incipient end of the world. Yet the index is 65 times higher than it was at the top in 1946 (and nearly 90 times higher than it was at the trough in 1949). And that doesn't count the compounding of dividends.

But where are the Armageddons of yesteryear? Vanished, of course: each wiped away, in its time, by a resumption of the inexorable progress of the free market—the essential human impulse to be, to do and to own—which is the organizing principle of an increasingly free world in the twenty-first century. You cannot separate global equity prices from the global economy for very long. And, as we've previously noted, the global economy is by far the freest and most dynamic it's ever been. **The advance is permanent; the declines are temporary.** In eight words, this is pretty much all you need to know in order to be able to stare down the bear.

4. THEY ARE THE REASON THE RETURN OF EQUITIES IS SO MUNIFICENT. The long-term compound return of large cap equity, lo these eighty-odd years, is 10.4%, and of small cap equity, 12.5%. The compound return of high quality long-term bonds is a hair less then six percent. What do you suppose accounts for the huge difference in equity and debt returns?

Why, equity volatility, of course: *it's because of bear markets*. The premium return is an efficient market's way of pricing in—of demanding an appropriate return for—the extreme unpredictability of equity returns from one period to the next. It would be difficult, for example, to imagine a two-year period in which bonds had a positive return of 20% one year followed by a negative 20% the next. *Bonds just aren't that volatile*. In equities, it happens all the bloody time. An efficient market knows that, and demands adequate compensation.

Be careful what you wish for. Do not pine, even in the most terrifying markets, for an end to equity volatility, because you are asking for the so-called equity risk premium to melt away. If bear markets subsided in frequency and intensity—if, in other words, equity volatility went secularly south—equity returns would fall away as well. I don't think that's what you and your clients really want. So embrace volatility: it's what's making patient equity investors (like me, and—I hope—you) financially secure.

It's now time to examine the 13 post-WWII bear markets, not at all as an academic exercise, but rather pursuant to the wise counsel of two of my heroes, Winston Churchill and Harry Truman. The former said, "The further we look back, the further we may see ahead." And the latter said, "The only thing new in the world is the history you do not know."

I'm using a table which records only price levels rather than total return, because *in extremis* that's how people tend to think: they simply forget about dividends. This will skew some of the turning points—for instance, on a total return basis, the first of these bear markets ended not in June 1949 but two full years earlier, in May 1947. But I've come to believe that we should show bear markets at their worst, so that no investor under our guidance can ever get the slightest false sense of security. Thus: behold the modern bear, red in tooth and claw:

DATES OF MARKET PEAK	DATES OF MARKET TROUGH	% RETURN	DURATION	MARKET PEAK	MARKET TROUGH
05/29/46	06/13/49	−30%	36.5 Months	19.3	13.6
08/02/56	10/22/57	−22	8.0 Months	49.7	39.0
12/12/61	06/26/62	−28	6.5 Months	72.6	52.3
02/09/66	10/07/66	−22	8.0 Months	94.1	73.2
11/29/68	05/26/70	−36	18.0 Months	108.4	69.3
01/11/73	10/03/74	−48	20.5 Months	120.2	62.3
09/21/76	03/06/78	−19	17.5 Months	107.8	86.9
11/28/80	08/12/82	−27	20.5 Months	140.5	102.4
08/25/87	12/24/87	−34	4.0 Months	336.8	223.9
07/16/90	10/11/90	−20	3.0 Months	369.0	295.5
07/17/98	08/31/98	−19	1.5 Months	1186.8	957.3
03/24/00	10/09/02	−49	30.5 Months	1527.5	776.7
10/09/07	10/27/08	−46	12.5 Months	1565.1	848.9*

*As of this writing.

(My source for this table, not that you asked, is Leuthold Weeden Institutional Research for the first 12 bears, and my own record of the most recent unpleasantness.)

I say again: this is no dry statistical exercise. *People lived through these events; they remember how scary these episodes were.* They just need to be reminded of how ordinary, how mundane, how quotidian crisis is—and how evanescent. This chart is, in the very best sense, a teaching tool. And I call the act of teaching with it *Lifeboat Drills.*

Now, anyone who has ever taken a cruise will know that lifeboat drills on a ship—learning how to put on your life jacket, learning how to get to your lifeboat station, *everything you need to know in order to be saved in the event of a shipboard disaster*—are conducted while the ship is still in port. This aspect of the analogy is particularly instructive, to wit: *you do not start doing lifeboat drills in the middle of the Atlantic, after* Titanic *has stopped to take on ice.*

Brothers and sisters: not just the best time but the only practical time to drill your clients in bear market realities—and I mean drill them to within an inch of their lives—*is smack in the middle of a lovely bull market, when there isn't a cloud in the sky.* **If you wait until a bear market to teach people about bear markets, you'll be too late.** Panic will already have begun to set in, and they will not be able to hear you. But by shaping the client's *expectations* through Lifeboat Drills, you can shape the client's *experience* the next time the bear attacks.

So you look again and again at the chart. And you see that—with utterly unpredictable randomness—the market has gone down an average of 30%, 13 times in 63 years, or about one year in five. Peak-to-trough, the average decline went on for about 16 months. At some point or another during those bear markets, America suffered economic and other disasters which seemed to portend the destruction of our system, if not—as in the Cuban Missile Crisis in 1962—of human life itself.

A president was assassinated, and another was shot very nearly to death. One party's putative presidential nominee and our nation's greatest civil rights leader were murdered within weeks of each other. Terrorists flew airplanes into the World Trade Center and the Pentagon, killing more people than died at Pearl Harbor. A hurricane totally devastated an area of our Gulf coast larger than Great Britain. And these are just some of the headline events.

Over 40 years of nuclear and then thermonuclear standoff, we faced down a monolithic enemy implacably committed to the destruction of our whole way of life. Today, that system is a bad memory, and our way of life—democratic capitalism—is energizing the whole world. Our workers are by far the most productive, highest paid workforce in history, and on any given day, more than 94% of everyone in America who wants a job has one. The financial net worth of the American household is greater than that of all the other households on the planet.

We will never be without problems, and some of them will be extremely serious problems. The point that this chart cries out to us—this endless chain of permanent advance punctuated by temporary decline—is that we bend, but we never break. And when we recover, we are more flexible, more resilient, more transparent and more entrepreneurial than ever. *The world does not end; it only appears to be ending from time to time.*

Once again: this is not cheerleading, nor starry-eyed optimism. *It is simply the above chart, rendered into prose.* History admits of no other conclusion. Remember the BIC's profession of faith: **"I don't claim to know exactly *how* it's going to turn out all right; I only know *that* it's going to turn out all right."** To believe otherwise is to say, "Maybe it *is* different this time." And that will surely lead to panic, thence to capitulation, and thence to the failure of the financial plan. *This time is never different*, and the more historical context you can supply to your clients, the easier it will be for them to understand that.

Uniqueness is one of the two delusions which prompt investors to view the apocalypse *du jour* as potentially terminal; the other is **extrapolation**. Say we're in a car, a hundred miles east of the Grand Canyon, and we're driving west at 60 miles an hour. Extrapolating our current direction and speed, it's clear that well within two hours, we will drive over the edge of the canyon, and hurtle fatally to the floor below. The internal logic of this conclusion is inarguable, but the larger hypothesis is absurd. We will not, in fact, keep to our current course and speed; realizing the danger, we will change our direction and/or stop the car.

Likewise, it's axiomatic that, on its present course, the Social Security system will soon be paying more in benefits than it is taking in, and that, as the baby boomers retire in huge numbers, their benefits will completely overwhelm contributions from current workers. Hence, the specter of Social Security "going bankrupt" is always a staple topic for alarmist journalism, when nothing more urgent seems to be going wrong.

The flaw is always in the assumptions: you can't, in fact, extrapolate the current system. One way and another, probably piecemeal over a long period, we're going to "fix" Social Security. We'll push back the retirement age, and/or index benefits to the cost of living instead of to wages, and/or raise payroll taxes, and/or means-test future benefits, and/or whatever. *In other words, as we get closer to the edge of the Grand Canyon, we'll change direction and/or stop the car.*

The extrapolation fallacy therefore rests on three false premises: that *today's singular crisis* is, all by itself, capable of breaking the American economy; that this crisis will continue in a straight line; and that we are powerless to alter its course. Since none of those things (much less all of them) is ever true, the catastrophist conclusions investors draw from them are never warranted. *Just look at all the past crises.*

The most important thing, for the advisor, is never to be put in the position of having to predict exactly how and when the apocalypse *du jour* is going to get solved *as a condition of his client staying in equities*. Assume that you will always be challenged by clients, in every bear market, along these lines: "Unless you can convince me that we're not going into recession/this subprime mortgage meltdown won't tank all the banks/this credit crisis isn't going to get much worse, I need to stop investing in/get out of equities."

We are under no obligation to predict any economic or market outcome, and indeed cannot. The moral high ground of our position is that all previous crises—many far worse than today's—have been successfully resolved, to the point where the American economy and its capital markets have resumed their unprecedented upward march. It is improbable in the extreme to assume that this time is different—historically, this time has never been different—*and all successful equity investing is based on historical probabilities, not remote catastrophist possibilities.*

This last point is terribly important, and most people miss it when they're in the grip of bear-market terrors that spin out in a malignant daisy chain of "What ifs."

For example, it is possible—if only in the sense that nothing is impossible—that some number of the major banks in the United States might become insolvent: that, overwhelmed by a tidal wave of bad loans, and unable to raise additional capital, they would be rendered incapable of meeting their obligations, and would fail. **This must be counted a *possibility*.**

And it may be assumed that such an event would tend to have a catastrophic effect on the financial system, and on the capital markets here and around the globe. Bank failures would probably spread; the cost of capital would soar as the credit markets seized up; companies that finance their operations with short-term borrowing would begin to fail; and the stock market would almost certainly crash, as investors fled to the safety of cash.

The critical question is: *granting that this chain of events is, however remotely, a possibility,* **what is the probability of it happening?** Here I believe we'd conclude that, for a multiplicity of reasons, it is improbable in the extreme.

First, as recently as the housing and banking crisis of 1990–91, banks had a near-death experience, and emerged far better prepared for such storms than they had ever been. Second, as the Federal Reserve demonstrated upon the failure of WaMu, it stands ready to take the most extraordinary measures to insure that the financial system continues to function—that a high-profile failure must not and would not be permitted to spread. Third, it seems clear from recent experience that staggering amounts of sovereign wealth, pent-up petrodollars and private equity funds are not merely willing but eager to participate in the recapitalization of America's banks at fire-sale prices.

One concludes from this that high-profile bank failures, while remotely possible, remain overwhelmingly improbable. You don't scrap a lifetime investing program—and liquidate a beautifully diversified, high quality equity portfolio at panic prices—over a remote possibility.

Granted, in the throes of bear market fear, the remotely possible may begin to *seem* probable to the investor. That, as we have seen, is exactly the moment that the BIC earns her fee, not just for this year but for a number of years to come. She does that through three media, the first and most important of which is her own unshakable *faith in the future*. Don't forget that all bear-market behavioral counseling is a battle of the advisor's faith against the investor's fear. And don't ignore the possibility that, in trying some disaster scenario out on you, the client may just be testing the depth of your conviction.

The second medium through which the advisor restores perspective is *history*: the implacable, undeniable implication of the bear market chart above. Which is that all bears are mortal; that they always die after a finite lifespan; and that the subsequent upward surge of equity values (and dividends) wipes out all traces that the bear ever lived.

The third and final medium for the BIC's triumph over panic is, as we've just seen, *the rational assessment of possibility vs. probability.* The purpose of this chapter has been to arm you with these three powerful weapons in the fight against investor panic, because panic is the ultimate saboteur of long-term investment success. That success can never be denied a person who invests—and who stays invested—in equities. We advisors get the investor into equities over a handful of days; that's the easy part. *The hard part is keeping him in equities over the next ten thousand days, and more.*

And our mortal enemy is not "underperformance," or recession, or the balance of payments deficit, or the entitlements crisis, or any other trend or event that's taking place anywhere except *between the investor's ears.* Our enemy is his own proclivity to panic. We must vanquish that impulse, or see the investor fail.

12

SUMMARY

᛬ Bear markets don't matter. The only thing that matters is how people respond to them: how surprised they are, a*nd what they think is happening*. Once again, what's going on in the investor's mind is immeasurably more important than what's going on in the markets, the economy, and the world.

᛬ The more you really know about bear markets, and the more of that financial and emotional intelligence you can systematically breathe into your clients, the less you need fear, because the less susceptible they will be to panic.

᛬ First, the technical definition: *a bear market is a period of time during which common stocks are returned to their rightful owners.*

᛬ Four things you and your clients must know about bear markets:

1. They are an essential, organic element of the never-ending cycle. As long as human nature governs economic activity, the economy will first overshoot and then undershoot its long-term trendline. Markets can only follow.

2. They're as common as dirt. Thirteen bear markets in 63 years works out to about one in five years. Average declines of 30%, sixteen months peak to trough. Look for eight in a 40-year working career and six more in a 30-year retirement. Common as dirt.

3. They are the temporary interruptions of a permanent uptrend. The first one started in 1946 at a market peak of 19. Thirteen ends-of-the-world later, the market's up 60 times. Get over it.

4. They are the reason for equities' premium returns. If the heightened volatility were not there, neither would the heightened returns be. It is an efficient market's way of pricing in the extreme unpredictability of equity returns in the shorter run. Don't just get over it; ***embrace it.***

- The principle of educating clients to expect, endure and even welcome bear markets is best thought of as Lifeboat Drills: you prepare people for a shipboard disaster while the ship is in port, and you drill people on bear markets during bull markets. If you start teaching people about bear markets after the ship hits the iceberg, a bunch of folks are going to drown.

- The world does not end; it only seems to be ending from time to time. No bear market is unique, none is fatal, and this time is never different.

- Extrapolation—"If we maintain this course and speed, we'll be fish food in the Colorado River in two hours"—is always a conclusion based on a false premise. We will change direction and/or stop the car. "No problem of human destiny is beyond human beings"—JFK. The problems invariably get solved by the humans. The cycle reasserts itself. ***Always.***

- Don't get manipulated into trying to prove something as a condition of somebody staying in the market.

- Any disaster is a possibility. None is a probability. Rational investors assess probabilities. If I considered all the terrible things that were possible on any given day, I'd probably never get out of bed in the morning.

- The BIC's three weapons against panic: faith in the future, history, and a rational assessment of probability vs. possibility.

We get people into equities in no more than five conversations over as many days. We then have to keep them in equities for the next ten to twenty thousand days, in a constant battle against their hard-wired proclivity to panic. That's what we get paid for, and we deserve to get paid for it on every one of those days.

13

BEAR MARKET Q&A:
TURNING VICTIMS INTO OPPORTUNISTS

THERE ARE, AT THE END OF THE DAY, ONLY TWO ways for client and advisor alike to process the experience of a bear market. One is as a victim; the other is as an opportunist.

There is, I suppose, a third way, best practiced by people who are finished investing, and/or living on their investments. And that, of course—to the greatest extent practicable—is just serenely to ignore it.

But for people who are still accumulating capital, a bear market is a heaven-sent opportunity to (you should pardon the play on words) **stock up** on the quality equity portfolios which will sustain their lifestyles in retirement and become their legacies to their children.

The lower the cost of your long-term portfolio, the higher will be your long-term return, and the sooner (everything else being equal) that you will achieve your financial goals. Thus, all rational wealth-builders should eagerly welcome a bear market. Sadly, most do not. This is yet another reason that the Behavioral Investment Counselor was sent into the world. And why long-term investment success, for most people, will prove to be impossible without the empathetic but tough-loving counsel of a BIC.

There is one overriding concept which becomes the lens through which the BIC tries to get his clients to view bear markets. Simply stated:

> DON'T THINK OF IT AS A "BEAR MARKET."
> THINK OF IT AS A "BIG SALE."

One year in five, on average, they mark down the prices of the great companies in America and the world an average of nearly 30%. That's always a particularly good time for long-term investors to be buying them. And it is a very bad time—unless you really, *really* need the money—to sell them.

There's only one drawback to these markdowns. It is, of course, that a sale is always occasioned by bad economic and financial news. Major markdowns usually attend upon major bad news. And whatever that bad news is—out of the rich, diverse tapestry that is the economic life of the world—journalism will seize upon it, and spin it out into a scenario for Armageddon. *That is, journalism will always—by isolating on whatever is wrong, and extrapolating it—make things appear much worse than they really are.*

Thus, the 24/7 financial news cycle functions as America's leading producer of the malignant fiction that this time is different. But that's not even my point. It's that all bear markets are an inseparable package of (a) *cyclically adverse economic/financial trends* (the reporting of which will always be hysterically overblown) and (b) *wonderful, life-forwarding sale prices on quality equity portfolios*—quite literally, the opportunity to buy them at prices no one may ever see again.

All anyone can do is to decide—consciously or unconsciously—to which of these two aspects of a bear market he is going to respond. (Again, a third option is simply stoicism: persistence in the knowledge that "this too shall pass"—on average, after little more than one complete turning of the leaves.) The mission of the BIC is to expend her finite reserves of time and energy helping people to focus on the right variable.

Specifically, the onset of a bear market should energize the BIC to concentrate on four career initiatives:

1. Helping long-term investors decide not to sell (note that I still refuse to use the word "convince"), and to persist in that decision even as prices continue to fall.
2. Helping long-term accumulators decide to keep funding their plan.
3. Encouraging long-term investors currently withholding cash from equities to commit it.
4. Prospecting actively for people who have been effectively abandoned by amateur advisors who proved incapable of dealing with a major market downturn.

Let's examine some approaches to the first three of these initiatives in the Q&A format, after which I'll suggest some specific methods of pursuing the fourth.

CLIENT: *I have to get out of the market. I can't stand it anymore. I'm down 25% in the last nine months, and* (fill in the name of the bearish guru *du jour*) *says it's still going lower, because of* (fill in the apocalypse *du jour*: the subprime mortgage crisis, oil, recession, terrorism, the balance of payments deficit, Iran's nukes, bird flu, the breakup of the Spice Girls, whatever).

BIC: *OK, let's get out.* (Silence.)

C: *Wait…you never talk like that. You're always long-term bullish. Do you mean it?*

BIC: *No, of course I don't mean it. I was just trying to get your attention.*

C: *Well, what's your advice?*

BIC: *Same as it was a year ago, and will be a year from now. You have an excellent financial and estate plan, if I do say so myself, and I do. You have a beautifully diversified portfolio, ideally suited to the achievement of your long-term goals. Right now that portfolio is backtracking, as it historically should about one year in five. You are, as you say, down about 25%, because the market's down 25%. If this is the average post-WWII bear market, do you know how much further it will fall?*

C: *I shudder to think.*

BIC: *If you think, you won't need to shudder, because the answer is: another five percent, measured from the top. Sell here, and it may feel good for a few weeks or even months. But then you'll start regretting it, and my guess is you'll go on regretting it for the rest of your life.*

C: *But suppose it isn't the average? Suppose it's worse?*

BIC: *Well, about half of them **are** worse, and half are less severe. In the absence of any ability to predict which this one will be—an ability no one consistently has—how do you make a strategy out of that?*

C: *You get the heck out, and wait for the economy to right itself.*

BIC: *That's the one strategy about which I can say with perfect confidence: **it never works.** By the time you and I are comfortably convinced that the economy is back on an even keel, the market will be long gone on the upside.*

> *Because the genius of the market is that it doesn't respond;*
> *it anticipates.*
>
> *Look, let's be candid, because we're friends, and friends*
> *tell each other the truth. You haven't got a strategy,*
> *you've got an impulse. And that impulse is real, and it's*
> *human, and it's very powerful, and it just says:* **make it**
> **stop hurting.**
>
> *It's very OK to feel that feeling. But for someone with your*
> *goals and your multi-decade time horizon, it's very much*
> **not OK to act on that feeling.** *Focus on your goals, fo-*
> *cus on your plan, turn the television off, stop pricing your*
> *portfolio, and let's talk again in 90 days.*

Note how very light the BIC kept this colloquy. It's psychologically very hard for two people in radically different emotional states to remain in a conversation. If one person is jumping up and down and screaming, "We're all gonna die! We're all gonna die!" while the other is calmly intoning, "No biggie; happens all the time; this too shall pass; probably close to being over, anyway," one of three things is going to happen: the hysteric is going to calm down, the calm person is going to get hysterical, or the hysteric is simply going to bail out of the conversation. The BIC just keeps talking calm, strategic, *non-predictive*, and above all *friendly* common sense, until the client calms down, or bails.

We spoke conceptually, a couple of chapters ago, about how to respond when called upon to deal with the ravings of some bearish third party. I want to expand on that issue, not just to refine your skill in this regard, but to use it as a window into an even greater strategic truth.

C: *I just downloaded this newsletter from* (fill in name of permabear). *He says* (fill in catastrophist prediction). *I need you to read it, and respond to it.*

BIC: *Why?*

C: *Why? Because if he's right, we have to get out of the market.*

BIC: *Can't really help you there. I won't know for sure whether he's right or not, any more than he does. Buffett said, "I have never met a man who could forecast the market," and I don't think he was being deliberately gender-specific.*

And, for the record, you never have to get out of the market, because to do so is almost certainly a long-term strategic mistake. I've seen people make that mistake and never recover from it. Sure hope you won't.

Dear reader, never underestimate the power of "Why?" It forces your interlocutor to expand and refine his issue/objection/question, it buys you time, and it suggests how imperturbable you are.

Moreover, in this specific example, "Why?" was the polite alternative to "No." No BIC worth his salt is going to waste his time reading, much less rebutting, the apocalyptic screeds that bubble to the surface of the blogosphere in bear markets, to the effect that the Rothschilds, the Elders of Zion and the Gnomes of Zurich are engaged in some fantastic financial conspiracy, or that Alan Greenspan was the second shooter on the grassy knoll.

The ironclad rule here appears to be simply: you never read this stuff, much less comment on it. *But observe the far greater, more comprehensive rule: that you cannot be drawn into a discussion of the market, because you're a planner, not a prognosticator.*

A planner doesn't—because he shouldn't—have a market viewpoint, as it can only distract him from his clients' long-term goals. You're running your portfolios off comprehensive financial plans, not off any economic or market outlook. And, by the way, long-term pessimism is counterintuitive. (It's also a crashing bore.)

Now, although it's somewhat obvious, let's consider the case of someone who wants to shut down "just for now" an equity accumulation program.

C: *We've been adding $6000 a month to my equity account, but this market is behaving terribly, and I don't think we should keep doing this.*

BIC: *I can't tell you how relieved I am to hear you say that. I don't think we should keep investing $6000 a month, either. Is there any way you can bump it to $12,000, before the sale ends?*

C: *Huh? No, I was talking about stopping…it's a terrible bear market.*

BIC: *Well, for some people, I suppose it is. But for you, it's a big sale. You can buy five fund shares for the same money that only bought four shares a couple of seasons ago. It's like a January white sale, or the auto industry's end-of-model-year clearance in August. The important difference is that you only get a sale this big on the great companies in America and the world around one year in five.*

C: *But…but…I'm only three years from retirement.*

BIC: *I know! It's really amazing; the timing is just perfect for you! You get to accumulate a whole lot of bargain-priced equity in the block of time before you retire. And then, in retirement—if history is any guide, and it's the only guide we've got—your account values and dividends will be cycling up again. I couldn't be happier for you.*

The ironclad rule, once again, is: for accumulators—and especially for accumulators on a relatively short fuse, like the chap in this example—it's not a bear market, it's a big sale. Indeed, for this fellow, it may be the last really big sale of his accumulating career, and the BIC enthusiastically hopes he doesn't miss it.

Note also that the BIC does not talk about stock prices; he speaks rather of a rarely-seen sale on *the great companies in America and the world*. People believe in great companies, even as they are terrified by stocks. And in times of great market stress, it becomes impossible for them to see that stocks and companies are the same thing, unless they are reminded of this by a wise counselor.

(By the way, if you think any of the examples I'm using in this book must be just imaginary, let me assure you that every single one, down to the last detail, is an inquiry I got from an advisor pursuant to the "Ask Nick" spot-coaching feature of my newsletter, *Nick Murray Interactive*. Remember the guy, a couple of chapters back, who objected that the advisor's fee—$15,000— could buy him and his wife another cruise? *Absolutely true story*. The guy above, who genuinely wanted to stop his equity accumulation program just three years from retirement because of a bear market? *Absolutely true story*.)

Now let's look at someone who has a significant amount of cash that must eventually go into equities, but which he is holding back because the market is going south. It's important that you understand the real psychological problem—as distinctly opposed to the stated financial problem—in such cases.

The investor *says* he's staying out because of some poorly thought-out potpourri of bearish snippets he's patched together, which suggest that the market has lower to go. You're not going to engage with this smoke, not just because you never debate the direction of the market, **but because you know that the stated issue isn't the real issue**—which is, of course, the very human fear of taking a big wad of cash and making a big mistake with it.

So what the BIC is going to try to do is get the investor emotionally unstuck, by suggesting a strategy of multiple entry points which have no particular financial relevance whatsoever, *but which give the client the opportunity to put in a little money at a time.*

C: *Aunt Sylvia left us $300,000, and we know we have to invest it in equities for our retirement at some point, but we can't put it in the market now because* (regurgitates whichever apocalypse *du jour* was the lead story on CNBC's morning program today).

BIC: *The S&P is 1200 today. Where do you think it's going? You see, you pretty much have to have a strategy; you don't want to be making decisions on impulse with a substantial sum like that, wouldn't you agree?*

C: *Well...uh...let's see...I think it's going to 1000. Give or take.*

BIC: *Perfect. Super. Just tell me what the strategy is if it doesn't get to 1000.*

C: *I guess I hadn't thought it through that far.*

BIC: *No problem. Let me suggest a strategy for getting the money invested carefully, gradually, and wisely, without your having to predict the market. May I do that?*

C: *I wish you would.*

BIC: *Put a third of the money in today. This hedges you out of the risk that the market turns somewhere in here, and runs away without you. If it doesn't, if it's still going down, you've still got two-thirds of your powder dry.*

           Halfway down from 1200 to your target 1000—at 1100—you put in a second third. Now you've hedged out of the risk that you were mostly right, but that the market just never got as low as you thought it would.

At 1000, you put in the last third. Your average cost is only 10% higher, but you didn't risk betting the ranch on a big number, and being wrong. What do you think?

C: *I feel like a huge weight's been lifted off my shoulders. I don't really know if the market's going to 1000 or not; I was just afraid of making a stupid mistake. This is the biggest windfall we'll ever have, and she was my wife's aunt, not mine, and...*

Wait; what if it never gets to 1000? What do I do if it turns around?

BIC: *Yes; that's the rub. You also need to pre-select a point at which you'll say: bear market's over; we've got to be in.*

C: *This is really starting to make my head hurt. Can I just ask what you'd recommend?*

BIC: *For a 55 year-old couple with 10 more years to work and 30 years to try to live on your investments—a total of 40 years? In equities, which are up more than 12 times in the **last** 40 years? I'd put all the money into your quality portfolios by nightfall...and then go out, have a transcendent dinner, and raise a glass to Aunt Sylvia...who certainly didn't leave you this money so you could agonize over it. That's what I'd do.*

C: *And not have to worry about it anymore. Of course; let's do it.*

Reader, I can't guarantee this happy an outcome every time you do this technique—which, for the record, I call "Splitting the Difference." But I can tell you that, more reliably than anything I ever tried or heard of, this will tend to get a cash-rich, fear-frozen investor moving again.

And the key to its efficacy—as in all the previous examples in this chapter—is simply that you never for one moment engaged in any discussion, analysis, prognostication or argument concerning the economy or the markets.

We conclude now with a five-part strategy which the opportunistic BIC will have in a can on a shelf in his office, ready to go at the instant that CNBC announces the official onset of a bear market: a close 20% below a previous high close.

Restrain yourself: don't implement this strategy after a 10%–15% market decline. Those come along as often as the crosstown bus, and as quickly reverse to the upside. You don't want to wheel up all this artillery and have nothing to shoot at; you'll only scare people, and end up looking like the BIC who cried wolf. Save this program until everybody's really scared—and amateur advisors are curled up under their desks in the fetal position.

1. SUMMON ALL CLIENTS AND PROSPECTS TO A BEAR MARKET REFRESHER COURSE. Have a cracker-jack seminar, built around the table of historic bears in the previous chapter, ready to go at a moment's notice. Keep it light, sweet, strategic and opportunistic. Do not under any circumstances get sucked into a discussion of current market conditions. *Testify to your faith in the future.* People will thank you for it, and never forget you. Because, in a season of crisis, yours may be the only positive voice they hear.

2. GO THROUGH YOUR ENTIRE ACCOUNT BOOK, AND ASK EVERY SINGLE PERSON IF HE COULD POSSIBLY ACCELERATE HIS ACCUMULATION PLAN, OR INVEST ADDITIONAL SUMS, "BEFORE THE SALE ENDS." I can't guarantee that you'll raise one additional dollar on the first pass-through. But again, people will have heard a positive, optimistic, unafraid opportunist. And they'll remember you.

What We Offer
A Cup of Coffee and a Second Opinion

When the markets turn as volatile and confusing as they have over the past year, even the most patient investors may come to question the wisdom of the investment plan that they've been following.

At (name of your firm), we've seen a lot of difficult markets come and go. And we can certainly empathize with people who find the current environment troublesome and disturbing. We'd like to help, if we can, and to that end, here's what we offer:

A cup of coffee, and a second opinion.

By appointment, you're welcome to come in and sit with us for a while. We'll ask you to outline your financial goals—what your investment portfolio is intended to do for you. Then we'll review the portfolio for and with you.

If we think your investments continue to be well-suited to your long-term goals—in spite of the current market turmoil—we'll gladly tell you so, and send you on your way. If, on the other hand, we think some of your investments no longer fit with your goals, we'll explain why, in plain English. And, if you like, we'll recommend some alternatives.

Either way, the coffee is on us.

*(Add your own verbiage here about how you wish
to be contacted, or how you propose to follow up.)*

Even if their assets under management are cyclically declining in bear markets, great advisors always use these periods to strengthen and expand their practices. Act while all around you are reacting—embrace bear markets as an opportunist, not a victim—and you can always do the same.

It sure beats sitting around waiting for the phone to ring.

13

SUMMARY

- There are only two ways to process the experience of a bear market. One is as a victim; the other is as an opportunist.

- Start by thinking of it not as a "bear market," but as a ***"big sale."***

- Bear markets are virtually always occasioned by genuinely adverse economic and/or financial events and trends. Journalism will seize on the negative, take it out of context, blow it all out of proportion to the economy as a whole, and extrapolate it right straight over a cliff. (One recent example: in 2008, surging exports added far more to economic growth than a depression in homebuilding took away. Journalism, which should always have been ritually pointing this out in the interest of balanced reporting, was silent on the good news and hysterical about the bad news.) Journalism ain't your friend.

- It takes genuinely adverse economic/financial events/trends to get you the kind of life-forwarding sale prices on quality equities that you get only about one year in five. The adversity not only begets the opportunity; ***the adversity is the opportunity.***

- In a bear market, the BIC focuses on four career imperatives:

  1. Helping long-term investors decide not to sell, and to persist in that decision even as prices continue to fall further.

  2. Helping long-term accumulators decide to keep funding their plans.

  3. Encouraging long-term investors currently withholding cash from the market to commit it.

4. Prospecting actively for people whose advisors turned out to be among the victims.

🔖 Point out to people who want to flee equities how close the market is to its historical average trough by the time they're ready to capitulate.

🔖 Again: do not read nor comment on catastrophist predictions. Even a stopped watch is right twice a day, and even permabears get a day or two in the sun one year in five. But long-term pessimists are always wrong.

🔖 Help people withholding cash to formulate a plan for deploying it as (and if) the market continues south. Plans are inherently anxiety-reducing, while impulses simply increase people's fear of being really wrong.

🔖 At the point where the market closes down 20% from a previous high, put into practice the following five-part plan:

1. Summon all your clients and prospects to a joyous, opportunistic bear market refresher seminar.

2. Prospect your entire account book for more money "before the sale ends."

3. Prospect your entire account book a second time, seeking introductions.

4. Prospect everyone you've ever prospected, looking for those whose advisor turned out to have clay feet.

5. E-mail the "What we offer: a cup of coffee and a second opinion" letter to the entire English-speaking world. People love it, and respond very strongly to it.

14

THE RETIREMENT INCOME CRISIS:
A BEHAVIORAL ISSUE

A PROSPECT HAS SUDDENLY CALLED YOU, OUT OF the blue, and asked to come in for a consultation about his income in retirement. He volunteered that he wishes to bring his wife with him. And he clearly if nonverbally communicated that he wants to do this sooner rather than later.

(Forgive me, but how many buying signals can you stand, all at the same time? You didn't call him; he called you. He asked to have his spouse present. And he is giving off a palpable sense of urgency. This is a principled-persuasion trifecta.)

On the appointed day—let us say next Monday—in they walk. And it is immediately clear whence comes this remarkable quickening of the process: *he's retiring a week from next Friday,* and he just couldn't put this conversation off any longer. He had to talk to *somebody*, and Emerson's Compensation exchequer somehow printed out your name. (You must have recommended something really, really good to some other prospect and been turned away, because—no question—here comes the payback that the Sage of

Concord and I assured you was awaiting your claim.)

That last datum about the prospect—*he put this off as long as he could*—should remind you of something very important. Namely, that retirement, and the need completely to change one's financial direction—from working and putting money away to not working and taking money out—*is the single biggest, scariest financial decision people ever have to make…and it involves the largest sum of money they will ever have to move.* Brothers and sisters, start firing up your empathy generator, here: the process that's just beginning as the couple walks in *is one part money to 19 parts sheer terror.*

You'd never know it to look at him, though. He's well if quietly dressed (as is she). Because you've trained yourself to look carefully, on first meeting prospects, at their leather and their gold, you see right off that his loafers and his watch say money, as does her engagement solitaire. He's all business, and he starts the conversation with a demand:

> PROSPECT: *We have $1.4 million in an IRA rollover, and I'll be getting $2.7 million from my company's 401(k) when I retire. That's the money we have to live on for the rest of our lives, and we have to invest it very carefully. So the first thing we want to know is: what is your firm's current market outlook?*

Now, if you're ever going to help these people, begin by observing all of the genuinely terrible things that are trying to happen here, just in the guy's 30-second opening salvo. (1) He tried to set the agenda, which isn't his to set. You're the neurosurgeon; he has the aneurysm; this is your meeting; you will be the one to set—or in this case re-set—the agenda. (2) Predictably, he set the agenda in the wrong terms: a market outlook, instead of a lifetime income plan. Strike two. (3) He is trying to set himself up as the arbiter of whether your and your firm's advice is valid, and that just isn't something you can allow to happen.

Remember: have some empathy for him. He's terrified—they both are—but he's a successful guy, with a lot of money, and he's used to calling the shots, and he doesn't know you, and he's trying to assert control, if only because he's afraid of what may happen if you get control. Hence his act. *And he's so good at this act—he's been doing it for so long—that he may not even be conscious of how terrified he is.* Now: realize that it's an act. And, without turning this into a test of manhood, start the conversation over again.

It may help if you remember one thing: *the odds are very nearly seven to one that this couple started out in life from absolute scratch, without two nickels to rub together.* That's what U.S. Trust found, when in 2007 it surveyed American households with a minimum of five million dollars of net worth, over and above the value of the primary residence. *Eighty-four percent of the respondents said they'd started with nothing.*

Be respectful of what they've accomplished—indeed, try to find out more about it—but don't be intimidated. *Try to see them as they were, not as they are.* I read an interview with Charles Schwab not long ago—a billionaire who's been rich since he virtually invented discount brokerage a third of a century ago—and he suddenly blurted out that his early life was so financially straitened that *his first bike was used.* And I thought: **Rosebud.** (Remember, from *Citizen Kane*?) Sixty years and several billion dollars later: *that used bike still hurts.*

Yes, your prospect is wearing Ferragamo loafers and a Patek Philippe watch, so you won't know that he had to drop out of college to start working, and it still pains him that he never got a degree. His wife's engagement ring really is lovely, but you won't know that she got it on her 35th wedding anniversary; when all her friends were getting diamond rings, she was married in a plain gold band, because that was all they could afford. (I understand these people because, as my newsletter subscribers know, I am these people.) *See us as we were, not as we are.* And, very gently, start the conversation over again.

BIC: *Well, gee, first of all, let me congratulate you on the success you've had in accumulating a significant retirement nest egg. There must be a very interesting story to it, and I would love to hear that story at some point. Until that day, please know that I respect what you've put together, and I respect its importance to the quality of the rest of your lives.*

Now: our firm's market outlook…that's what you asked about, wasn't it? Well, we must have one, I suppose, and it must be around here somewhere. I confess I don't pay much attention to market opinions—ours or anyone else's—because it's essentially irrelevant to what I do.

I'm a retirement income planner, and I work to make sure that my clients' retirement income can continue to support their lifestyles through three decades of retirement. *What the market's doing at any given moment doesn't usually have much effect on lifetime income, so I mostly tune it out.*

But you're certainly entitled to know what our outlook is, and I'd like to excuse myself, and go find it for you. Just before I do that, though, may I ask you a question of my own, that I think may be even more important? (Prospects nod assent.)

As you sit here today, looking out at the balance of your lives—*of both of your lives*—are you highly confident that your income will always be enough to sustain your lifestyle? Or have you become at all concerned that, at some point during your retirement, you might actually start to run out of money?

This is the issue; indeed, this is the crisis. I'm never as sure as CNBC seems to be—because they use the word so often and so loosely— that we're ever actually having a subprime mortgage "crisis," or an oil "crisis," or a bird flu "crisis." But I can tell you for absolute certain that we are having—and for a number of years to come will continue having—*a retirement income crisis*. That crisis presents advisors with a career-making opportunity.

This question—the only one that matters—is the moment of truth. How people respond to it will tell you almost immediately whether the conversation has any chance of going anywhere. That's because there is, in its essence, only one true answer to it:

"WE'RE JUST NOT SURE."

The great importance of this answer is twofold. First, it's the pure truth, even if it's a truth that the prospects haven't faced before. For reasons that will become obvious as we examine the psychology of today's retiring Americans, they are exaggeratedly focused on issues relating to their *principal*, when they should be infinitely more concerned about the continuing adequacy, over three-decade retirements, of their *income*. Thus, it's not just that they aren't sure what the answer to The Great Question is: they've never been able to frame the question itself.

The second reason this answer is so important is that, if she doesn't hear it—or something mighty close to it—the BIC can be reasonably sure that the prospects are in the process of disqualifying themselves, right before her very eyes, in the first five minutes of the conversation.

If he keeps perseverating about the market, or if he goes off on a tangent about how they can't take any risk, or that they want a lot of guarantees, or what your fees are—*or anything other than "We just don't know the answer to that question; can you please help us figure it out?"*—chances are this interview may already be winding down. You can only help people who are willing to be helped, by you, now.

Let's proceed under the assumption that the folks heard their cue, and had the grace to answer honestly: "Gosh, that's the real question, isn't it? And the truth is, we're just not sure."

BIC: *Then let me suggest that we defer any discussion of a market outlook, just for a while, until we get to the bottom of the retirement income issue. Because this is the big one: not just the most important concern, but almost the only concern. Does it make sense to you to proceed in that way?*

Presuming that the prospects assent to this, you will note that the BIC has now totally recovered control of the agenda, and has reset it in his own intensely focused terms. While he retains control of it—which means: until the folks are either fully invested or have bailed out—there will only be one issue on the table, back to which you will see the BIC constantly bringing the conversation: **retirement income.**

P: *Fine, but I'm not sure what we do next.*

BIC: *We do two things. We may not get to them both today—in fact, in a way it might be just as well if we don't, because the first one **really** gives you a lot to think about, and there's no harm done if you just want to take some time to think it through.*

*The first thing I need to do is to just sort of sit quietly with you and talk through the whole idea of retirement income—what it needs to do as your cost of living rises throughout your retired lives, and **how** we get it to do what it needs to do. My part of that conversation takes about 15 minutes, but at the end of it, you literally know everything I know about retirement income. When I've said my piece, we can either call it a day, or sort through any questions you immediately have,*

Assume we end up, at the end of that first stage, pretty much on the same page: that we share a perception that the basic challenge is safeguarding your purchasing pow-

er. In the second step, we do a detailed analysis of all your sources of retirement income, and project your living expenses through three decades of retirement. We make sure we can keep the trend of your income well above the trend of your living expenses.

If we can, fine, and if it looks like there might come a point where we can't—where the expenses might be starting to outrun the income—then we have some decisions to make. But if that problem is coming, we want to make sure we see it coming years and years before it gets here, so that we have options and choices—and time to think about them.

The big thing, for me, is that we don't do anything in a hurry, and don't do anything you don't fully understand and agree with. If this works out the way I think it will, we're going to be working together for 30 years. I know retirement is coming at you really fast, but I don't want you to feel pressured by it. I'll make sure you have all the time you need to make good decisions.

Reader, that whole lovely, warm little speech—from "We do two things" until the end—takes all of two minutes. And, although I don't know how I'd go about proving this to you, I can pretty much guarantee that **no financial advisor has ever spoken to them this way in their lives**.

Remember that the perception after which I order all my other perceptions is that these people are terrified—indeed, possibly so terrified that they have no idea how terrified they really are. They are, as we have seen, facing the biggest financial decision they will ever have to make, with the largest sum of money they have ever had. (Assuming this guy was born 60-odd years ago, in the 1940s, he doesn't have more money than his parents thought he would have; he has more money than his parents **knew was in the world**. Don't think he's not conscious of that, and don't think it doesn't add to his anxiety, because it does.)

So all we're really trying to do at this early stage is to get their heart rates back down to normal resting levels. I've had pre-retirement interviews—and I'm sure you have, too—where, after the first five minutes, I thought I was going to end up having to do CPR on the dude. That's just how stressful the subject is. And you are certainly not going to get any valuable information across to them until you can settle them back down.

> P: *If you seriously believe you can get us knowing everything you know about retirement income in fifteen minutes, you can certainly start anytime you're ready.*

And here the curtain goes up on your rock-solid presentation, "Everything Everybody Really Needs to Know About Retirement Income in 15 Minutes:"

> BIC: *OK, start timing me. If I go over 15 minutes, blow the whistle on me!*
>
> *First, the headline, the umbrella point, the organizing idea:*
>
> **Financially speaking, retirement is essentially an *income* problem.**
>
> *You would think this would be intuitive, but a lot of people I deal with start off thinking that it's somehow a **principal** problem. But you don't ask, on any given day, "Do I have enough **principal** to gas up the car, and to renew my prescriptions, to pay my greens fees and go out to dinner?" You very properly ask, "Do I have enough **income** to do those things today?" That's why we say that, day in and day out, year in and year out, **financially speaking, retirement is essentially an income problem**. OK so far?*

> P: *Income problem; got it.*

BIC: *Good, because this may only take 15 minutes, but that's because it only has one topic: **retirement income**. Now, the second point—the subheading, if you will:*

The two most important things in a retired lifetime— and these have to be purchased every day with your *retirement income*—**are** *dignity* **and** *independence,* **as you define those values.**

And in my experience, dignity and independence just get that much more important to people as they grow older. Would you agree?

P: *Dignity and independence, not becoming a burden to our children, real important, no argument there. Awful soft and mushy so far, but you're less than two minutes in.*

BIC: *Exactly. Now I think that when you really embrace those two ideas—it's an income problem; specifically, do you always have enough income to purchase dignity and independence as you define them—the problem suddenly subdivides into two issues, which I call the **duration of retirement income** and the **direction of retirement income**.*

*The **duration** issue asks: **does these people's retirement income last** at least **the balance of both of their lives?** And, equally important, the **direction** issue asks: **does these people's retirement income continue to grow** at least **at the rate their cost of living is growing for the balance of both of their lives?***

OK, prepare to stop the clock: are you completely and totally convinced that those are the essential questions about retirement income: does it last the rest of your lives, and does it keep rising to offset increases in your cost of living...so that, as dignity and independence become more expensive to buy, you have that much more income to buy them with?

P: (very quietly, looking right at his bride for the first time) *No, there's no need to stop the clock. I know you're right. I don't know why I never could organize it that way in my mind, because when you say it, it seems so obvious. But we're with you.*

BIC: *Great, because I'm happy to tell you that we're over the hump, and on the downhill side. Do you know the only way in the world to be absolutely sure you're getting the right answers…about retirement income or anything else?*

P: *I'm going to guess it's: make absolutely sure you're asking the right questions.*

BIC: (beaming) *Exactly! And we just asked **both of them**: the only two right questions, about the only two things that count. Retirement income that lasts two lifetimes; retirement income that keeps pace with the cost of living.*

       On the way downhill, we'll look at the four elements of the answer. They're probably fairly obvious to you now, but I just want to tick through them quickly. I call them the four epiphanies, and they tell us how we're going to get the right answers.

       Epiphany #1: *This is the defining fact of the rest of your lives, and it dictates the other three epiphanies. Simply stated, you're both 62—average retirement age in this country.*

       And you've told me you don't smoke. So I can tell you, from the modern mortality tables, that if all you are is the average couple, one of you has 30 years to live. Which means that the duration and direction questions now have a number on them: does the retirement income last for at least 30 years, and does it rise to offset increases in the cost of living for at least 30 years?

*Epiphany #2: The fundamental challenge to income over a 30 year, two-person retirement is **erosion of purchasing power**. Which is really just a highfalutin' way of saying: **every year, everything you need to buy will cost more**. And I have an easy way for you to remind yourselves of this.* (Hands them a card, on which are juxtaposed a 1980 Summer Olympics 15-cent postage stamp and a 2008 Frank Sinatra 42-cent stamp.)

At a 3% annual increase in consumer prices—the rate that's prevailed over the last 80-odd years—it's going to take $2.45 in the 30th year of retirement to buy exactly what one dollar bought in the first year. Which leads you directly to:

*Epiphany #3: The only rational goal of a retirement income portfolio is to produce a dollar income that rises through the years at more or less the rate that your dollar cost of living is increasing. Only in that way can your income keep pace with your expenses. And only **that** way can you expect to continue to be able to purchase dignity and independence in retirement, as you define those things. Which makes it acutely important that you realize:*

*Epiphany #4: For purposes of this discussion, there are really only two kinds of investments you can choose: **fixed-income** investments, and **rising-income** investments. Those are about the only kinds they make. And without belaboring the obvious: the more fixed-income investments you take into 30 years of a rising-cost world, the greater your chances of running out of money. Whereas the more rising-income investments you take into a rising-cost world, the greater your chance of keeping pace.*

And what are fixed-income investments? Well, there are CDs, bonds, mortgages, fixed annuities...things you've al-

ways thought of as being "safe," but right now I'm hoping you're not so sure. And where, most reliably, does a rising income come from? **From the constantly rising dividends of the great companies in America and the world.**

Now, I'm very nearly finished—and well within my 15 minutes, I see—but I do need to add a full-disclosure item. You're going to find this out from somebody, sooner or later, so I want you to hear it from me now.

You see, throughout this little presentation, I've been talking about trying to build an income stream that rises at more or less the same rate as the cost of living rises. Truth is, the great companies in America and the world haven't done that, historically. **They've raised their dividends at about one and a half times the rate consumer prices have gone up.** *And of course, the great companies have appreciated in value over long periods of time—but I promised I'd only talk about income.*

Those are the big truths I want us to focus on. And I'm sure you have some questions, yes?

Income is the issue in retirement investing. Specifically, income must rise to offset increases in the cost of living. Bonds don't do that. Equities—to be referred to, in conversation with anyone near retirement, as *the great companies in America and the world*—do, and then some, through the medium of their constantly rising dividend stream. Dividends have consistently (and quite steadily) grown at a significant premium to increases in consumer prices. (Note that I never use the word "inflation," any more than I ever say "stocks." And may we be struck dead if we ever use the dreaded phrase "the stock market.") ***Dividends are the moral high ground of equities.***

We now return to the conversation in progress, where the inevitable is just about to happen.

P: *You can't be saying...can you...that we should invest our retirement nest egg in...**the stock market**?*

BIC: (with magisterial calm) *I'm outlining, as clearly and completely as I can in the time allotted, your options. Which, it seems to me are: take an essentially fixed-income bond strategy into 30 years of rising living costs. Or embrace the constantly rising dividend stream, as well as the gradually increasing values, of the great companies in America and the world. And earn a total return that has historically exceeded the rate at which the cost of living has gone up by a very comfortable margin. Simple as that.*

P: *But...but...but...but...*

BIC: *Good heavens, man, spit it out!*

P: (with a keening wail) ***Stocks are too risky!***

DEAR READER, THE GAME IS AFOOT!

14

SUMMARY

- Respect and empathize with the emotional stress of the retirement income planning decision, especially when prospects have procrastinated about it. It is the single most important financial decision people ever make, with the largest sum of money they'll ever have to move. Assume this decision-making process is one part money to nineteen parts terror.

- Nothing even remotely productive can happen until you are in firm control of the agenda, which must be set (or, when necessary, re-set) in terms of one issue and one issue only: *retirement income.*

- Try to see your retiring prospects not as they are now—probably at the very peak of their affluence—but as they were. Chances are nearly seven out of eight that they started with nothing. Sometimes, to paraphrase Freud, a Rolex is just a Rolex. But a lot of times, it's a way of compensating for the pain of having found a used bike under a 1940s Christmas tree.

- Looking for an elevator speech? Can't imagine why, but try this one on for size: *"I'm a retirement income planner, and I work to make sure my clients' retirement income is always enough to buy them dignity and independence in retirement, as they define those things."*

- As soon as possible, ask the only question that matters: "As you sit here today—looking out over the entire balance of both of your lives—are you highly confident that your income will always be enough to sustain your lifestyle? Or have you become at all concerned that, at some point during your retirement, you might actually start to run out of money?"

❧ At retirement, there is only one financial issue: is the money going to outlive the people, or are the people going to outlive the money. As gently (but firmly) as possible: refuse to be drawn into a discussion of anything else. This is the issue that must be faced.

❧ Once the agenda is firmly set in terms of income (as distinctly opposed to principal), speak gently and reassuringly about your intention to take your time and talk through the issues slowly and carefully, not rushing to any conclusions, nor forcing any precipitous decisions. Describe how you are going to proceed, so the prospects will have that much better chance of following you. ***Keep them comfortable.***

❧ Financially speaking, retirement is essentially an income problem. And the two most important aspects of a high-quality retirement are dignity and independence, as your prospects define those blessings. ***But dignity and independence have to be purchased every day with—you guessed it—one's retirement income.***

❧ When prospects embrace the conclusions in the paragraph above, the retirement issue subdivides into two questions: duration and direction. The duration question asks, "Will these people's retirement income last at least the balance of both of their lives?" And the direction question asks, "Will these people's retirement income continue to rise throughout their lives at more or less the rate their cost of living is rising?"—such that, as dignity and independence cost more with each passing year, there will be that much more income with which to purchase them.

❧ These are not merely the two most important questions; they're the only right questions. Affluent people tend to think that legacy planning is equally important. But if they don't get the answers to these two retirement income questions right, there aren't going to be any legacies: Mom and Dad will have run through all the money.

ℒ When you've gotten the only two questions that mattered framed right, the answers present themselves in four epiphanies:

1. The joint life expectancy of a non-smoking couple of average retirement age (62) is 30 years. This not only puts a number on the only two questions that matter, it dictates an investment time horizon.

2. The central financial challenge in a 30-year two-person retirement is erosion of purchasing power. At three percent trendline inflation, it will cost about $2.45 in the thirtieth year of retirement to buy what one dollar buys in the first year.

3. The critical goal of a retirement income portfolio—and perhaps the only rational goal—is the production of a dollar income that rises through time at about the same rate the dollar cost of living is rising. Taking a purely fixed-income investment strategy into 30 years of rising living costs would be tantamount to financial suicide.

4. There are, therefore, only two classes of investments available to the retirement income investor. They are fixed-income investments and rising-income investments. Fixed income derives essentially from debt securities: CDs, money market funds, bonds and the like. Rising income comes from the constantly increasing dividends of the great companies in America and the world. (The shares of the great companies also appreciate over time—another potential source of income—but never mind that.)

ℒ When you finally accept and embrace the idea of defining true safety in terms of the preservation (and even accretion) of purchasing power in retirement, you see that equities are much safer than bonds.

§ "Stocks are too risky" is merely an announcement by the prospect that he hasn't yet grasped the cosmic truth of the paragraph above. Do not try to "convince" him. Simply work to cut off all his lines of retreat, until he faces the truth or bails out.

15

RETIREMENT INCOME Q&A:
FACTS VS. FEARS

THE MAN WHO JUST EXPRESSED, WITH PASSION AND conviction, the belief that equities are too risky to hold in retirement is, as we observed, 62 years old. That means he was born in 1946, the very first year of the fabled baby boom.

As I write, the broad equity market in the United States, as denominated by the Standard & Poor's 500 Index, stands at around 1200. A year or so ago, it was well over 1500. *It ended 1946 around 18.*

In other words, equity values have risen, just within the lifetime of the prospect to whom you're speaking, something like 70 times, even during the most recent bear market. Yet here he sits, big as life and twice as terrified, asserting that "stocks are too risky." Forget about "overcoming the objection" for a moment, because that so completely misses the point. There really is only one appropriate response we can make—carefully, gently, therapeutically—and it isn't a statement at all. It's a question.

WHERE DID YOU GET THAT IDEA?

When you encounter a person who espouses a deeply held belief *which is totally contradicted by all the realities of his own life*, this is the first thing you want to know.

What you usually find out is that the misapprehension originates in the person's early life, and specifically in the view of the world that he absorbed from his parents.

A person born in the mid-1940s is the child of two people who grew up in the 1920s—by far the most prosperous, hopeful, expansionist, downright optimistic decade in history up to that time. It was the age of miracles: automobile ownership became widespread, electrification brought radio into the home, Lindbergh flew the Atlantic and Babe Ruth hit 60 home runs. Everyone who could work was working, and—in cities, if not on farms—at wages no one had ever seen before. Interest rates went down, taxes went down, and the stock market soared. Today was better than yesterday, and tomorrow would surely be better than today.

And then it was all taken away. Suddenly, without warning or explanation, the worst economic depression in history enveloped these people, and darkness lay upon the land for a decade. Thus our prospects' parents learned: optimism and progress—even hope for a better tomorrow—were all lies. The world was a dangerous place, full of loss, lack and limitation. Everything you had might, and probably would, be snatched away from you in a moment. It was a worldview of insecurity and fear—and as soon as they started having children, that generation began teaching them those "lessons"—out of love, and a desire to make sure the children would not be hurt the way they were.

Take care not to conflate all the Depression generations—to lump them together in your mind. In a few years, you will begin counseling pre-retirees who were born in, say, 1955. Their parents were born around 1930...*and were therefore probably always poor.* Indeed, it may have taken them a few years even to realize that they *were* poor, because everyone around them was just as poor. (An acquaintance of mine, born in 1933, says that he had no idea his whole neighborhood was poor until he started kindergarten, in a school about a mile away, and saw children there who were wearing new shoes.)

Growing up poor was certainly a searing experience, and surely the 1930s generation burned its terrible stories into their children's minds, as well. But it was a totally different experience from that of the parents of the 1940s generation—my generation. I gave an extended version of this hypothesis to an advisor audience not long ago, and afterward a fellow about 40 years old came up to me, almost in tears, and told me that, for the first time in his life, he understood his grandmother (who must have been of my mother's generation). She always said, to her children and grandchildren, "You will never know what it is like to have it all, and then have it all taken away."

The generational problem you encounter when talking to my contemporaries is compounded by the way our culture uses language. We universally define our concepts of financial "risk" and "safety" only in terms of *principal*—whereas it's a matter of financial life and death to the couple sitting before you that they learn, before it's too late, to see the real risk as *the erosion of purchasing power*. They are being stalked not by the risk that they will lose their money—a risk which, over 30 year periods, is historically nonexistent—but by the risk that they will outlive it.

Finally, there is the issue of *time perspective*. Financial journalism, in its obsessive quest for news at the expense of truth, compresses its audience's focus down to whatever is going on *right this minute.* In this way, it robs people of the ability to *think through time*—to match long-term historical perspective to their own very long life expectancies. This leads people to confuse *risk* with *volatility*, which is a critical mistake.

In the short run, equities are extremely *volatile*: why, one day alone, in October 1987, they went down 23%. But are they, in any long-term historical sense, *risky*? After all, as I write—late in the fourth bear market since that day about 20 years ago—equity prices are nearly five times higher than they were the night before that epic decline. And over 30 year periods—roughly equivalent to a modern two-person retirement—equities have never produced a negative return.

The cost of living, by contrast, has never—in the 62 years the prospects in the example we're using have lived on the earth—stopped going up. *And the only reasonable assumption we can make is that it never will.*

Thus, by producing a fixed income from a fixed-dollar asset, bonds are said by the culture to be "conservative." But all they're conserving is the same fixed number of paper dollars, whose purchasing power is constantly eroding. In that sense, bonds may be "conservative" of principal, *but they are relentlessly corrosive of purchasing power.*

Equities, on the other hand—shares in the ownership of the great companies in America and the world—may be very volatile in price over short and intermediate time horizons. (Again, that is only a comment on their prices; their dividends never stop going up.) But volatility is not risk: the temporary contractions in equity prices are always overwhelmed in time by the resumption of their permanent uptrend. Finally, as we saw earlier, volatility—the unpredictability of equity prices over shorter periods—is both the reason for, and the driver of, equities' premium returns. *For all their evanescent volatility, it is equities which are truly "conservative" of purchasing power.*

In my book *The Excellent Investment Advisor* (1996), I synthesized the case for embracing equity volatility in this parable:

Imagine your car breaks down in the middle of Death Valley. If somebody doesn't come along soon, you'll die. Then, as the sun beats down and your tongue begins to swell…just when you're at wit's end…there on the horizon is an oncoming car. It's getting closer…closer…and…oh, no! It's *green. You hate green cars!* So… you wave the guy on.

"VOLATILITY" IS THE GREEN CAR.

So when any child of Depression-era parents—be he war baby or boomer—assures you that stocks are too risky, know that it is some variation of this toxic soup that you are dealing with: (a) the deep insecurity and fear that his parents breathed into him in earliest life; (b) mistaking short- to intermediate-term volatility for long-term risk, and not assessing equities' performance by the light of their own very long life expectancies; and (c) seeing risk and safety solely in terms of principal, when they should be immeasurably more concerned with risks to—and the safeguarding of—purchasing power.

All my years and all my professional experience—again, added to the fact that I actually am one of these people—confirm that the best approach to their misapprehension is much more therapeutic than educational. That's because you're dealing primarily with irrational fear more than with ignorance of the facts. And the first thing you learn about fear in this business is that it's extremely hard to reason with: untreated fear is powerful enough to filter out all the facts in the world.

That explains my first response to the statement that "stocks are too risky." It isn't a graph, or a chart, or a statistic; it isn't even a declarative sentence. It's the empathetic and therapeutic question, "Where did you get that idea?"

Remember: the burden of proof isn't on you—which is good, since you can't prove anything. Your mission is to try, within reason, to help people unpack the suitcase of fear that they've been dragging around all these years, and which they most recently dragged into your office, about half an hour ago. This is yet another reason that the earliest and strongest impression you want to convey to prospects is of trustworthiness much more than of competence. You may be a Nobel laureate in economics, but they're never going to unpack that suitcase in front of someone they don't instinctively trust.

Unfortunately, financial advisors aren't usually trained to deal with the pathology of irrational fear. Fear is the proverbial elephant in the living room, and advisors seem to be trying to look everywhere but at it. I think that's a mistake. My approach is to speak directly to the presence of the elephant, so that at some point the folks may feel comfortable telling it to leave the room. (Of course, this approach runs the risk of moving the folks to order you to leave their elephant alone, and to give *you* permission to leave the room. But at least you'll have called the right question.)

Here is a bouquet of comments you can consider making to the issue of fear—not all at once, and not in any particular order, but one or two flowers at a time, in season.

- I want you to be assured that I can feel your fear on this issue—I'm clear that this is very troubling to you, and I'm not taking it lightly.

- Please know that I respect your fears on this subject, in the same way that I respect all your feelings—just because they **are** your feelings, and I sense how very real they are to you.

- I want you to know that your fears will always be safe in this office—that you always have someplace, and somebody, to go to with them.

- I don't mind your being afraid, in and of itself. The decisions you have to make are very important, and they can be very scary. *I guess what I'm mostly trying to do is to make sure you're afraid of the right thing*, which isn't losing your money, but outliving it.

- Mr. and Ms. Prospect, I assure you, from the bottom of my heart, that you're entitled to your own fears. But (*very, very gently*) you're not entitled to your own *facts*.

This last observation is the nub of the problem, and—whichever of the other flowers you present to the folks during the interview—this may be the one you always want to end up with.

BIC: *And that's where I think we are. The values of the great companies in America and the world have gone up something like 70 times in your lifetime—indeed, some of these companies pay dividends that are higher than their prices were 30 years ago—yet you so clearly fear them.*

If there were some rational alternative that solved your problem, I would gladly take you to it. But there isn't. You will fight off your rising living costs, over the next 30 years, with the rising dividends and values of the great companies, or you will run out of money. I can see no third outcome.

So here we sit, with the fears and the facts pretty much lined up against each other. And I can see a lot of potential for all three of us to get hurt in the crossfire. So, if I may, I'm going to call time out. Unless you insist, we're not going to make any big decisions today. We'll put whatever monies you have now into a money market fund—which I always think of as a decision not to decide today—and just keep talking this through. Would it give you some comfort to do that?

I wasn't trained to do anything remotely like that, and I'm betting you weren't either. Instead, I was trained—when someone said "stocks are too risky"—to say, "No, they're not," and to hold up the Ibbotson chart. At some point, I noticed that this argument never worked, so I tried empathy. That only worked sometimes. But by then I had accepted—emotionally as well as intellectually—that, like all advisors who don't quit, I was playing heaven's own original numbers game. And therefore I'd found that **"sometimes" is infinitely better than "never."**

I hope you can imagine how immensely relieved these prospects simply must be when you tell them they don't have to decide anything today (which in their minds may still be code for: *he isn't going to try to sell us anything today).* You cannot operate successfully—that is, no matter how good your intentions, you can't force anything good to happen—*beyond the point up to which they've learned to trust you.* Take your time, and work to increase not their level of intellectual knowledge of equities but rather *their capacity to trust you.*

> BIC: *So what I'd like to do—if you would—is to go back to the point at which the facts and the fears got crosswise to each other. I've already mentioned what I think are some of the key facts: values up 70 times in your lifetime, and up five times just over the course of the last five bear markets. Dividend growth clicking along at a big premium to increases in living costs. Total return of the broad market more than three times the rate of increase of the Consumer Price Index.*
>
> *Over to you: as I started to ask a while ago, where does your fear—the sense that equities might be "too risky"—come from?*
>
> P: *Well, everything we've ever read and heard says that, as you approach retirement, you should phase out of equities and into bonds, for safety and income.*
>
> BIC: *Yes; isn't that awful?*
>
> P: *Sorry; what is your point?*
>
> BIC: *Simply that the conventional wisdom is still the same as it was a generation ago, when retired life expectancies could be measured in single digits—when nobody could even imagine the average retired couple having to fight off three decades of rising living costs.*

*But, as I hope you saw from my little speech about retirement income, the big issue in **your** retired lives is implicit in the fact that, for 30 years or more, **every year, everything you buy will cost more.** Your income either rises to offset those increases in living costs, or you run out of money. The great companies in America and the world produce rising dividends and values; bonds fix them. No safety there that I can see.*

P: *But equities are so much more volatile than bonds.*

BIC: *Yes. Up, mostly.*

P: *You lost us again.*

BIC: *I was simply observing the fact that big moves in equity prices are overwhelmingly to the upside. Equity returns have historically been positive four years out of five since WWII. As I mentioned, there've been five bear markets since October 1987—including the biggest decline of the postwar period. But today, values are about five times higher than they were just before the '87 crash. **And of course, dividends never for a moment stopped going up.***

If you retired on October 1, 1987, and invested in equities, you've enjoyed a genuinely spectacular increase in your income, your net worth and your lifestyle—despite the "volatility." If you invested in bonds and other fixed-income investments on that day, I'm guessing you're out of money, because your living costs have doubled, near about. (A first class postage stamp cost 25 cents on October 1, 1987; do the math.)

If that's what equity volatility does to long-term returns, I say bring it on.

P: *OK, but we're retiring now, and we need income. Bonds just yield a lot more than stocks.*

BIC: *(Sadly) Rainfall, snowfall…*

P: *I'm sure that must mean something to you.*

BIC: *As a matter of fact, it does. You see, the long-term total return of the great companies in America and the world—or as they're called on CNBC, the S&P 500—is 10% and change, while the return of corporate bonds is just a hair under 6%. Equities have a much higher total return than bonds, but bonds do—as you say—have a higher current yield. Which must just mean that equities appreciate in value a whole heck of a lot more than bonds do.*

*My point is that **both the dividend and the appreciation of equities are there to provide income to you.** You would never say, about the well in your back yard, "I can only draw out the water that got in there from snowfall; if I draw out the rainwater, I might get in trouble." Rather, you'd say, "Rainfall, snowfall: **it's all water**. And as long as I'm drawing out less water than the total of what nature is putting back in, I'm going to be just fine."*

And by the way, not to clutter up a beautiful analogy with a lot of pesky facts, but: today's dividend from the S&P is something like 12% of your going in-cost on October 1, 1987. So my advice to anyone who's staring at 30 years of rising living costs is twofold.

(1) Rainfall, snowfall: don't look at current yield; look at total return. (2) Don't look at where equities' yield is today; look where it's probably going, if history is any guide, over your retired lifetime.

P: *But what about those years when it neither rains nor snows, and the water in the well is evaporating? What happens when we go to take out 6%, say, in a declining market?*

BIC: *Always a possibility, and one year in five, a probability. There are a number of ways to handle it, but the simplest is just to keep two years' living expenses in a money market fund, so that you can cut back on—or turn off completely—your withdrawals from equities for a year or two, when equity values are going temporarily south (even as dividends are still rising!).*

When you let people unpack their suitcase of fear, these are conceptually the sad, tattered misperceptions you find: old conventional wisdom; definitions of risk and safety left over from their mom's and dad's retirement, but no longer suitable to theirs; volatility confused with risk; too much concern with losing money and not enough concern about outliving it; thinking of income only as yield and ignoring total return. Remember, they've had that old suitcase under their bed for a very long time.

Bushido: the BIC just sits there, calmly and effortlessly batting these objections aside, until they're all gone…*or until the real objection rears its ugly head:*

P: *Well, if you must know, we lost an awful lot of money in the tech disaster in 2000-2002. Had to put our retirement off for another five years. We're never going to go through that again.*

This kind of objection is a lot more common than you may think, and it always centers on the same psychological quirk: the refusal to accept responsibility. **The prospect is still blaming the market for something *he* did.** In this case, he put too much money into a speculative fad, and then panicked out of it when it inevitably cratered. Not to put too fine a point on it: *that wasn't the market's fault.* The BIC is going to handle this one very gingerly:

BIC: *I'm genuinely sorry that happened to you, and I can well understand that it still hurts. But did you ever hear what Mark Twain said about a cat who once walked on a hot stove?*

P: *Can't say as I have. Bet you're going to tell us, though.*

BIC: *With your permission, I am. He said that a cat, having once walked upon a hot stove, would never walk on a hot stove again. **Nor on a cold stove.** He was talking, I think, about trying to learn too much from any one experience. And that might apply to the situation you describe.*

I'm hearing you say that you invested a lot of money—maybe too much money—in the tech bubble. And that when those prices declined catastrophically, you sold. Now, maybe if there were any justice, you'd have earned a pass: for your trouble, you would be exempted from 30 years of rising living costs in retirement. But there is no such pass. You still have to fight off 30 years of rising living costs, and a well-diversified portfolio of quality equities is still the only practical way to do that.

*Let the experience you had teach you not to invest heavily in a speculative fad; I'm all for that. Don't let it teach you not to invest in equities at all, because that's cutting off your nose to spite your face. Carry your pain and anger about the tech experience to **that** conclusion, and you'll run out of money in retirement. Coldest stove ever. You don't want to do that.*

With this empathy and tough-love, with this quiet but inarguable logic—and maybe with my book for clients, **Simple Wealth, Inevitable Wealth,** thrown in to seal the agreement—you will get even us children of Depression-scarred parents into an appropriate equity weighting. The trouble then will become: keeping us in equities.

The older we get, the stronger our proclivity to panic may become. Accept this, and deal with it as best you can. I don't like to leave this essentially upbeat discussion on a downer, but in the interest of full disclosure: you have to be prepared to see some small percentage of us go over the side.

You will, of course, marshal all the rebuttals you learned in the chapters on bear markets. You will remind people that the impulse to get out is always strongest when the decline is all but over. You will admonish them that to get out and then get back in opportunely, you have to be right twice, which is both financially and psychologically all but impossible to do. But some people will still insist on getting out.

C: *I lost $85,000 last month!*

BIC: *Good heavens, **how?***

C: *Just look at my statement from **your** firm!*

BIC: (Heaving a huge sigh of relief) *Gee, you really had me scared there for a minute. When you said you had **lost** money, I was afraid you meant you sold something, and I didn't know about it. **Because selling when your investments are down is the only way you can create a permanent loss in a well-diversified portfolio like yours.** If you haven't sold—and thank God you haven't—all you have is a temporary decline.*

C: *I never know what you're talking about anymore! I have to get out before I lose any more money!*

BIC: *Can I have a maximum of 60 seconds, to say a maximum of three things?*

C: *Sixty seconds! No more!*

BIC: *Time me. And please take a couple of deep breaths. (1) Your account, which was at about $3 million, temporarily declined a little less than 3% last month, as the general market did. Eighty-five thousand dollars is a meaningless number, other than as a percentage of your investments; using the dollar amount is, if you'll allow me to say so, just a way of whipping yourself up. (2) Maybe this is going to turn out to be the one year in five the market sells off meaningfully. Maybe it's not. In either event, the decline will be temporary, your dividends will continue to grow, and the decline will be much more than made up in the years to come. (3) Turn the television off, stop looking up your portfolio online, and put your next couple of statements in a drawer.* **You don't deserve to have to worry this much at this point in your life; but you have to make a decision to stop.**

C: *Thanks very much for nothing! Sell everything and send me a check!*

BIC: *Here's what I'm going to do. I'm going to take your account to my manager/supervisor/senior partner, and have him/her enter the orders. That's simply because I'm absolutely convinced that this is* **the worst financial decision you have ever made, or ever will make, in your life.** *If any commission or other compensation comes to me from these transactions, I will refuse it. If they won't let me refuse it, I will donate it to your favorite charity in your name. Now:* **tell me once more that this is what you want to do.**

Some percentage of the time, this will talk him in off the ledge… for the moment. The rest of the time, he'll bail. So be it.

A while back, I stated an ironclad rule: that once your best advice had been turned aside, you never again initiate contact with a person. (It's OK if he calls you, but you may never call him. If you do,

I'll know, and I won't be happy.) Here is a bear-market corollary, not just for retirees, but for everybody:

> ONCE SOMEONE PANICS OUT OF EQ-
> UITIES AGAINST YOUR ADVICE, NEVER
> GIVE ADVICE ON HOW TO GET BACK IN,
> OTHER THAN "BUY IT ALL BACK AT THE
> MARKET RIGHT NOW."

Engage in no discussion—of the economy, the markets, or multiple entrance-point strategies. Either he takes full responsibility for what he did, acknowledges that he should never have gotten out, and is back in the whole portfolio by nightfall…or suggest he find another advisor.

I leave you on this historical high note. Alexander Hamilton was sworn in as America's first Secretary of the Treasury on September 11, 1789. I invite you to pick any date since, note the market's close, and then look ahead 30 years to the day. In other words, examine *any and every 30 year rolling period that is now complete.*

> YOU WILL NOT FIND ONE 30 YEAR
> ROLLING PERIOD IN WHICH EQUITIES
> PRODUCED A NEGATIVE RETURN—
> EVEN IF YOU IGNORE DIVIDENDS.

And therein lies the tragedy of my generation—a generation programmed from earliest life to think only of guaranteeing its principal—and which is therefore doomed to run out of money in retirement, and to die destitute and dependent upon its children.

It isn't just that we're going to be killed fighting the wrong dragon (principal loss, as opposed to extinction of purchasing power). No, our tragedy is even greater than that: *we are going to be killed fighting a dragon that doesn't exist.*

15

SUMMARY

⚜ Equity values have risen about 70 times in the life of an average retiree who is sitting before you, big as life, affirming his passionate belief that "stocks are too risky." There is only one possible response: "Where did you get that idea?"

⚜ Usually, when someone clings to a deeply-held emotional belief that is contradicted by all his own life experience, he acquired that belief in earliest life from his parents. It is axiomatic that people retiring today were acculturated by a generation whose defining economic/financial experience was the Depression. Horror stories of the Depression, spun out into family myth, are the usual suspects. And of course the creation myth of the Depression is that it was caused by the stock market crash of 1929.

⚜ There are, however, two different generations of Depression survivors: those who remember the hopeful era before it, and those who were born into it. The former generation was scarred in a completely different and terrible way; theirs are the children of the 1940s—war baby and early boomer alike—who are retiring today. When you start counseling pre-retirees born after 1955, to pick a year, their parents will have been born into the Depression. Always find an opportunity to ask, "What was the attitude toward money in your home when you were growing up?"

⚜ People who were acculturated by Depression survivors always overestimate the risk to their principal, and underestimate—if they do not completely ignore—the risk to their purchasing power. Secondarily, they equate equity market volatility with principal risk. These two key misperceptions form the essence of the BIC's challenge.

In the lifetime of today's retiree, three fundamental economic/ financial trends are the dominant realities: (1) The cost of living has never stopped going up, and probably never will. (2) The dividends of the great companies in America and the world have never stopped going up, and indeed have surged in this century, as corporate cash flows have surged. The dividends of many great companies are in fact higher than the share prices were 30 years ago. (3) The values of the great companies have increased upwards of 70 times, because corporate earnings have grown nearly as much; values have appreciated nearly four years in five.

Bonds may be "conservative" of principal, but they are relentlessly corrosive of purchasing power. Equities, for all their evanescent volatility, have proved to be truly "conservative" of purchasing power.

Speak directly to prospects' feelings of fear. Give them permission to feel their fears, while encouraging them not to act on their fears. In the end, gently assure them that they're certainly entitled to their own fears, but they're not entitled to their own facts.

Never make a major investment decision when the fears and the facts are still lined up against each other. Someone will get killed in the crossfire, and my money's on you.

Respect the amount of bad information with which your prospects are constantly bombarded. It is still the conventional wisdom—and therefore wisdom's opposite—that as people approach retirement, they ought to switch out of stocks and into bonds. This is planned financial suicide. You know that; I know that. But it may take the folks a while to get there. Keep showing them the stamps; *keep refusing to be drawn into an argument.*

You don't have to go back to the ancient history of 1946 to demonstrate the miracle of equities. Since they topped out in August 1987, there have been five bear markets in equity prices, *and they recently stood nearly five times higher.*

§ Rainfall, snowfall: total return, not current yield, is the standard by which an asset class's income potential should be judged.

§ Keep two years' living expenses in a money market fund when you're drawing income from equities. That way you can cut back on, or even stop, your equity withdrawals until a declining equity market rights itself. Or you can cut back on your living expenses. Or you can get a nice part-time job. In heaven's name: anything but bonds. Bonds in a 30-year retirement, as Chuck Yeager said about punching out of a supersonic aircraft, are like committing suicide to keep from being killed.

§ Probe to see if a prospect's antipathy to equities isn't just him blaming the market for something he did—like a speculative binge and/or panicky capitulation. Tell him Mark Twain's cat story. If he doesn't crack even a little smile at that, throw him out. He's a bore, and you must at all costs eschew bores.

§ You can get panic-prone people into equities. The difficulty is keeping them there. In the moment of truth, tell people what you believe: that panicking out of a declining market is the only way to create a permanent loss in a well-diversified equity portfolio, *and that they are about to make the single biggest mistake of their financial lives.* Then stand aside.

§ Once someone has panicked out, never call him again. If he calls, offer no economic or market commentary, and do not suggest a strategy for getting back into equities, other than "Buy the whole portfolio back, at the market, right now."

§ Since Alexander Hamilton became the first Treasury Secretary, there has never been a 30-year rolling period—starting any day you like—where equities have produced a negative return, even if you ignore dividends. That's the real tragedy of today's so-called "risk-averse" retiree: not that he's going to be killed fighting the wrong dragon, but that he is going to be killed *fighting a dragon that doesn't exist.*

§ Speak truth to that fear. Never stop speaking it. And you will go straight to the top of this profession, there to remain as long as you like. Such is the goal of this book; such is my wish for you.

AFTERWORD

GEORGE WASHINGTON WROTE THAT, HAD THE BRIT-
ish wished to pursue his army as it retreated into winter camp
at Valley Forge, they could easily have done so by following the
bloody footprints in the snow. And I would have you know that, in
my own way, I've left blood on virtually every page of this book.

Every mistake I identify, and work to help prevent you from making, is one I've made times without number. Every principle, skill,
script, and response technique I offer you is one I labored slowly
and painfully to develop. I learned from my mistakes infinitely
more than from my successes, if only because the former so hugely
outnumber the latter. Nothing came easily to me in this business;
anything of value you find in this book was built, brick upon brick,
in a process that is, well into its fifth decade, still unfolding.

Yet however slowly the great truths of the craft of advice came to
me, *they did come*, for one reason and one alone: *I did not give up.*
(In the interest of full disclosure, this last statement is narrowly
true, but importantly incomplete. The whole truth is that there
were times—as the average common stock declined 70% between

1968 and 1974—when I wanted to give up. But I had—and have—the good fortune to be married to the best and most courageous person I've ever known. And she wouldn't let me.)

I was so terrified for so long—of money, of people, of all the things about investing that I didn't know—that I would write out everything I was going to say to a prospect, word for word, and practice it on Joan. After a while, as I began to identify questions and objections that recurred often, I would take them to the big producers in my firm, and write down the answers they gave me to use.

These scripts and responses ultimately filled two notebooks. The notebooks became a career. Nearly twenty years ago, the career turned into a book called *Serious Money*, which was really just a long letter to the rookie I had been almost a quarter century earlier. *Serious Money*—half a dozen books later—has turned into the book you're holding in your hands.

I am, in my blood and bones, a personal financial adviser just like you. You are not going through anything I haven't gone through, although you are probably handling it better than, for years and years, I did. Any success I've had is wholly attributable to persistence. Indeed, I would state, as the cardinal tenet of this profession, that ***all success begins as the failure to fail.*** Just get up in the morning; try to think of one thing you learned yesterday; resolve to learn just one more thing today; go out there and fight again. ***Never give up.***

As for me: in the words of the 84-year-old Michelangelo, *"Ancora imparo"*—I'm still learning. I have the great good fortune to be living (and investing) in the age of miracles. I'm blessed with the ability to use whatever modest gifts I have for writing and speaking in the service of all the other financial advisors of my time—and to prosper thereby. I believe I was sent into the world to do this work, and I derive an almost inexpressible joy—as JFK defined joy—from doing it.

There is, I believe, no profession nobler than ours. When we do it well, we enrich the lives of people who may long outlive us—indeed, perhaps people yet unborn. Believe in the nobility of what we do; believe in our limitless capacity to intervene decisively in people's lives. Believe in your unique opportunity to do well—for yourself and the people you love—by doing good for others. Press on. "It matters not how slowly you go," said Confucius. "It matters only *that you do not stop.*"

APPENDIX A

TWO LETTERS AND TWO CHARTS

———

LETTER SEEKING INTRODUCTIONS. As I suggested earlier in this book, advisors seem to labor under two obvious misapprehensions. First is that clients give—or ought to give—advisors referrals. This has never been true, and never will be. *Happy clients, and only happy clients, may—if properly approached—do so.* (I repeat that this is yet another reason—if you needed another— never to keep an unhappy client.)

The second misconception is that what you should be looking for is referrals. It isn't. As my mentor of many years past, Marvin Brown, taught me: we should be working to get not referrals but *introductions*, which are so much more powerful.

Here is a letter seeking introductions. Tweak the fact pattern to fit your situation, of course, but examine the essential premises: (1) that the advisor seeks introductions only if the client is completely happy, *and that he wants to know immediately if the client is not.* And (2) that the advisor *will be following up*—that this letter merely states the circumstances in which the advisor will seek introductions. *The letter is not an end in itself. It is a statement of intent.*

Dear Client:

We hope this letter finds you well, and thriving.

As you may know, we started our firm five years ago with the goal of serving a very finite number of affluent families/households with the level of comprehensive financial planning which they need, and deserve.

We now find our practice about halfway to our goal, in terms of the number of people we feel we can serve effectively. And our momentum seems to be accelerating.

At this rate, we can begin to see the day approaching where we will need and want to stop accepting new clients. Between now and that point, we would much prefer to establish relationships with the friends and colleagues of our existing clients. We enjoy working with you, and are sure we'd enjoy working with people you like and admire.

To that end, we will soon begin asking you—in our conversations with you and at client appreciation events specifically organized for this purpose—to introduce us to such people…provided, of course, that you are perfectly comfortable doing so.

We don't expect—and frankly don't think we deserve—introductions to be made by our clients unless you are satisfied and happy with the service we provide you. That's why, as we begin these conversations, we will urge you to tell us, freely and candidly, anything you feel you need or even want from us that we're not already doing. Your satisfaction remains our primary goal.

But if we're serving you in the ways you hoped and expected we would, then—and only then—we will ask you to introduce us to someone you believe should be similarly served. We treasure our relationships with our clients, and seek only to serve a few more people like you.

We welcome any suggestions which this letter sparks, in terms of people we should be talking to. And we look forward to following up this letter personally with you.

Thank you for your time and consideration. And thank you for giving us the opportunity to serve you.

Sincerely,

THE "PITA" LETTER. Every year on your birthday, give your-self the priceless gift of self-esteem: fire your biggest PITA (an ac-ronym, of course, for Pain In The Neck). This is the person who has given you, since your last birthday, the most trouble—however you choose to define "trouble," which could be anything from pa-perwork problems to fee carping to second-guessing your invest-ment recommendations to just making your skin crawl when you hear his (or her) voice.

This will almost always be a substantial account. It may even be—as it was for me twice in my early struggles—your very biggest account. Let me tell you something you may unconsciously know, but about which you may be in denial: *he knows how important the business is to you.* That's why he thinks he can get away with all his passive/aggressive behavior.

You don't need this business. *You need your self-esteem.* The negative, hopeless message you send yourself when you submit to the subtle abuse of a PITA is, "I have to hold on to this busi-ness, even though it causes me so much pain, *because I cannot replace the business; I can't do better than this.*" That message is self-reinforcing. Its effect may appear to be a vicious cycle, but it's actually a downward spiral. In killing your self-regard, it is killing your career.

Stop the madness. **Fire your biggest PITA.** It is the best birthday present you could give yourself.

Moreover, do it with class, grace and style. Don't unload on the PITA all the pent-up rage, pain and frustration he/she has forced you to swallow throughout the relationship. That's what a passive/aggressive wants. (Then he'll say, "You took it the wrong way.")

The following letter defuses all the drama by putting you in the position of taking responsibility (but certainly no blame) for the failure of the relationship. It firmly but non-argumentatively closes the door. Now all you have to do is make sure the door stays closed:

never take another call from the PITA, because he will just try to sweet-talk you into taking him back, while he figures out how to make your life ten times more miserable than he did before you tried to fire him.

Dear (name):

I'm in the process of effecting some important changes in my business and my life. To that end, I've been reviewing all my client relationships.

In thinking about our business relationship with each other this last year or two, I've reluctantly concluded that I will never be able to serve you in the ways you seem to need. That being the case, it seems unfair of me to try to retain your account, and I'm therefore resigning it.

I have asked (name and/or title) to be in touch with you, with a view to finding you an advisor whose capabilities are better suited to your needs than mine are.

[Or, if you have no intermediary whom you can call in: When you have found an advisor better suited to your needs than I am, please have him or her contact me directly to facilitate the transfer of your account(s). I promise to give the transfer process my closest personal attention, as you surely deserve.]

I thank you for all your past business, and wish you every future success.

Sincerely,

CHART: THE MUTATION OF RISK THROUGH TIME. This is simply a conceptual graph which you can toss off in a conversation with a prospect/client. It doesn't have to be denominated in exact time or percentages, not least of all because it can't be.

First draw a simple graph; make the north-south axis **RISK** and the east-west axis **TIME**, thus:

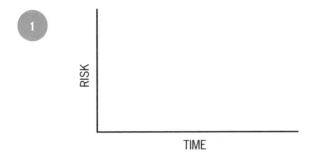

Then start by graphing the progress of the obvious "risk," which is principal loss. I think we would all agree that over very short periods of time the principal risk of equities is astronomical. Why, one day twenty-odd years ago the American equity market lost 23% of its value between sunup and sunset. So we're talking huge short-term risk.

As you say this, make a big dot on the chart, as follows. You see that, because it's very low on the **TIME** axis, the dot is very high on the **RISK** axis.

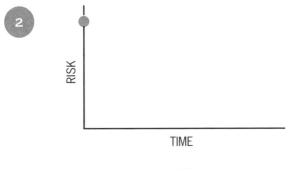

But almost immediately a funny thing happens. With the passage of time, the risk of holding equities historically declines, quite literally to zero. (Jeremy Siegel says there's never been a 17-year period in history in which stocks, with dividends reinvested, have produced a negative real return.)

Now, there's nothing sacred about 17 years (any more than your potential short-term loss is limited to 23%—or any other number). So the graph is illustrating a concept (indeed, as you'll see, two concepts); it's not predicting or calibrating the future.

The concept is simply that, over some period of time, the risk of holding equities falls all the way to zero...and stops there, because it can't go any lower. (This last point may seem so obvious that it needn't be mentioned, but it's about to become very important. Just watch.)

Illustrate the decline of principal risk to zero as follows, and then label the resulting bar:

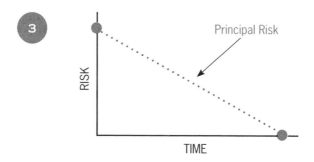

Now, let's look at the **other** risk of your economic life—the risk that does **not** decline but only keeps rising, without limit, for as long as you live (and then goes on rising throughout the lives of your heirs). That is the risk of the loss of your purchasing power—the risk that your cost of living will outrun your income.

In the short run, purchasing power risk is exactly the opposite of principal risk, in this sense: while short-term principal risk is astronomical, short-term risk of purchasing power is virtually nonexistent.

What is the chance that you'll walk into the supermarket tomorrow and find that a diversified basket of your household needs is markedly more expensive than it was today? I would say that risk is close to zero. So let's start graphing this risk literally at zero, by putting our starting dot right where the axes meet:

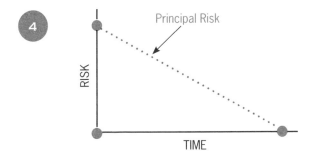

Here, though, we find that with each passing day the risk of losing our purchasing power—through the slow, steady increase in the prices of nearly all the goods and services we consume—***rises*** over time. But unlike principal loss risk, ***it has no finite limit***, other than the days allotted to us and to the loved ones who will survive us.

So when we graph the progress of purchasing power risk—which is the last step in this visual presentation—our chart ends up looking like this:

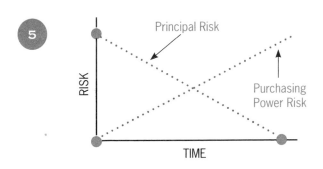

CONCLUSION: Principal risk, even if you *can't* distinguish it from volatility, has nowhere to go but down over time, as it mutates into purchasing power risk (or, more accurately, loss), which marches inexorably upward through the years, without limit.

CHART: THE TRAJECTORY OF LIVING COSTS IN RETIREMENT. Many people go into retirement with enough fixed income to meet their living expenses *at that point*—a datum from which they derive an ominously false sense of security. They ignore the fact that while their income is static, their living costs are dynamic—trending ever upward, to the point where living costs will begin to exceed income by an ever-widening margin. This very simple conceptual graph charts this effect.

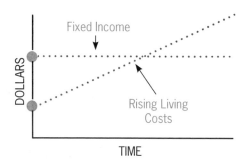

(Many of you already have—and I suggest that you aggressively use—software that enables you to put hard numbers on this phenomenon: to project when increasing living costs will cross over the fixed income line, using some agreed-upon rate of cost of living increases. Then, assuming that principal has to be withdrawn to fund the income shortfall, you can project the year in which the folks will run completely out of money. Your ability to show people the precise mathematics of outliving their income will be a critical career skill as the number of people retiring surges in the years ahead.)

APPENDIX B

BIBLIOGRAPHY AND RESOURCES

THE ONLY WAY YOU CAN FAIL TO BE PROPELLED TO the top of this profession by the truth of this book is if you stop prospecting. The primary if not dominant cause of failure in the retail financial advisory profession is prospecting anxiety. This is a purely emotional/behavioral issue, and can only be solved behaviorally. At an important juncture in my career, I found the work of the behavioral psychologist Aaron Hemsley to be immensely helpful to me. Aaron's work is systematized and carried on today in the personal behavioral coaching offered by his daughter, Darci Hemsley Brown. Darci can be reached directly at ahinfo@aaronhemsley.com.

I'm not generally a fan of "how-to" books in our business, if only because so many of them seem to be written by people who never did. Two wonderful exceptions—terrific books by supremely successful practitioners who are also great guys—are Roy Diliberto's *Financial Planning: The Next Step* and Bob Fragasso's *Starting Your Own Practice.* (Bob's book may appear to be just for advisors who are going independent. It's not. It's for everyone who wants to build a thriving business, and then to run it like a business.) To me, both of these books are must-reads, rich in practical insights and great human warmth.

One reason a lot of advisors never seem to get their arms around the broader operations of the capital markets is that they don't know enough economics. The Teaching Company (www.teach12.com) offers, at this writing, two very useful college courses in several formats. Professor Tim Taylor's basic economics course is an indispensable overview, and Professor Robert Whaples's course on modern economic issues is pointed at headline issues like health care, entitlements, oil, climate change, immigration and taxes. Both courses are extremely practical and helpful to the harried advisor.

If you would prefer to read a very non-technical book on this subject, I highly recommend Thomas Sowell's *Basic Economics*.

Beyond that, I just think that the more steeped you are in economic and market history, the more valuable an advisor you must become in the long run. The best one-volume history of the American economy is John Steele Gordon's *An Empire of Wealth*; Gordon also wrote a useful one-volume history of our capital markets called *The Great Game*. The latter is long out of print, and I fear that the former is on its way, but you can usually find used copies online.

The classic study of the financial cycle is the late Charles Kindleberger's *Manias, Panics and Crashes*. It's by no means an easy read, but every advisor should study it carefully. A more anecdotal survey of some of the great bubbles and crashes in history is Edward Chancellor's *Devil Take the Hindmost*.

Four great biographies, taken together, serve to frame an economic and financial history of the U.S. from the great post-Civil War expansion well into the twentieth century. They are Jean Strouse's *Morgan: American Financier*, Ron Chernow's *Titan: The Life of John D. Rockefeller, Sr.*, Joseph Frazier Wall's *Andrew Carnegie*, and David Cannadine's *Mellon: An American Life*. The Cliff's Notes version might be Charles R. Morris's *The Tycoons*, about Morgan,

Rockefeller, Carnegie and the underappreciated Jay Gould. Les Standiford's *Meet You in Hell: Andrew Carnegie, Henry Clay Frick, and the Bitter Partnership That Transformed America* is an additional read that's both serviceable and fun.

A recent book on the first great financial crackup of the twentieth century—with echoes well into the recent unpleasantness—is Bruner's and Carr's *The Panic of 1907: Lessons Learned from the Market's "Perfect Storm."* Maury Klein's *Rainbow's End: The Crash of 1929* is a fine treatment of that subject. And, since its first publication forty years ago, John Brooks's *Once in Golconda: A True Drama of Wall Street 1920–38* has always been a sentimental favorite of mine. (Brooks's *The Go-Go Years* is also excellent on the markets of the 1960s.)

Amity Shlaes's *The Forgotten Man: A New History of the Great Depression* is the one absolutely indispensable treatment of our long national nightmare, its true causes, and the ways in which the New Deal's ceaseless, quixotic experimentation and vicious class warfare made it orders of magnitude worse than it should ever have been.

The best way to understand what went wrong in the 1970s (excluding dividends, the equity market in 1982 was where it had been in 1966, and the average common stock declined 70% from 1968 to 1974) and then went right in the 1980s is the late, lamented Robert Bartley's *The Seven Fat Years*, out of print but readily available used.

Charles R. Morris wrote something to the effect that it takes genuinely brilliant people to produce an epic financial disaster. Never was this more pointedly true than in the case of Long-Term Capital Management, a hedge fund created by—among others—two future Nobel laureates. It became the largest hedge fund in the history of the world up to that time—until, in the summer of 1998, it zeroed out, threatening to take down the world financial system if it tried to unwind all its spectacularly losing positions. This saga—a cautionary tale to which too few people were paying attention less than ten years later—is brilliantly told in Roger Lowenstein's *When Genius Failed*, another must-read.

Two good histories of the tech bubble of the late 1990s are *Dot. con* by John Cassidy, which focuses on the development of the Internet, and Lowenstein's *Origins of the Crash*. Both should be read for their historical perspective; their rather silly prescriptions for avoiding such excesses in the future may safely be ignored. The epic fraud of Enron – if anybody still cares – is masterfully reported by the two people who blew the lid off: McLean's and Elkind's *The Smartest Guys in the Room*.

But by far the most important book to come out of the tech bubble and crash is a brutally honest memoir: David Denby's *American Sucker*. Not only should you read this indispensable book, but you should give it to clients, especially as markets rise.

Richard Bookstaber's *A Demon of Our Own Design: Markets, Hedge Funds and the Perils of Financial Innovation* was almost eerily prescient when it was published in April 2007; it demands to be read today. Also useful, or at least very entertaining, is Nassim Nicholas Taleb's *The Black Swan: The Impact of the Highly Improbable*.

William J. Bernstein's *A Splendid Exchange: How Trade Shaped the World* is the most accessible one-volume history of world trade I've ever seen, or expect to see. It documents the fact that the impulse to trade is essential to man's makeup, and that trade has been globalizing the world economy for almost as long as we've been human.

NICK'S RESOURCES

FOR YOU AND YOUR CLIENT

FOR THE ADVISOR

NICK MURRAY INTERACTIVE. This newsletter and "spot coaching" resource is entering its ninth year; it's among the longest-running, highest-circulation advisor newsletters in the financial advisory profession.

Each month, subscribers receive online a newsletter about eight pages in length, filled with practice management essays; long-term strategic commentary on economics and markets; advisor-client scripts; capsule reviews of recommended books and other resources (speeches, articles and the occasional academic paper); and most months a "Client's Corner" essay, which subscribers may reprint in their own client/ prospect communications. An especially popular feature of the newsletter is constant commentary rebutting scare headlines and other declinist journalism: it's the antidote to the apocalypse *du jour*.

The newsletter also features selected, anonymous "Ask Nick" Q&A from the "spot coaching" service which is available only to subscribers. This aspect of **Nick Murray Interactive** offers subscribers coded e-mail access to Nick for situational coaching on specific client/prospect issues, which he answers *as time permits*. (During the first eight years, 90% of "Ask Nick" inquiries were answered within 48 hours.) In many cases, subscribers have said that one key answer to one critical situational question was worth an entire year's subscription cost.

You may subscribe, or simply download a sample issue of **Nick Murray Interactive**, by visiting www.nickmurray.com, and clicking on "Newsletter."

FOR THE CLIENT:

SIMPLE WEALTH, INEVITABLE WEALTH. This very readable, totally non-technical book for clients —written to them by Nick in the first person—is, according to publishing industry statistics, one of the most successful privately-published books of the last ten years.

In fewer than two hundred conversational pages, Nick suggests a common-sense, goal-driven, long-term approach to equity investing, and constantly reinforces the point that **clients will not make it without an empathetic, tough-loving** *behavioral coach*. In exactly that way, this may be the only book of any consequence in the English language which tells clients they absolutely must have a financial advisor.

Many advisors report that **SWIW** has helped them win significant accounts, has prevented many clients from panicky capitulation, and even that it serves as their "operations manual"—telling new clients, as they board The Ark, what to expect from the advisor on their voyage.

ACKNOWLEDGEMENTS

MY LIFE IS MY FAMILY AND MY WORK. I AM UNUTTERably blessed by the extent to which the two intersect.

My wife Joan, as I revealed in my Afterword, gave me the courage—her courage—to persist through the very dark early years of my career. If today you are deriving any benefit from my work, you needn't thank me: thank her. Joan also brings to my business and my life the priceless ability to see things as they are, not as I would want them to be, and I always end up wishing I'd listened to her sooner. A gifted entrepreneur in her own right, she knew when to hold 'em and when to fold 'em, and in doing so contributed mightily to our family's fortune.

The most astute critic and most acerbic editor of my written work has always been my firstborn daughter Karen. A brilliant and highly-sought-after financial writer and editor in her own career—in addition to being David Dickerson's loving wife and Rebecca's and Will's supermom—Karen's style, taste and insight inform every chapter of this book. Any and all remaining errors are mine.

The Nick Murray Company's books are kept—accurately, insightfully, and in her spare time—by my daughter Joan, a trainer and healer of athletes on all levels, and an athlete herself who walks—or should I say runs, bikes and swims—her talk. Joanie might deny it, but when a certain Academy award-winning actress injured her neck in a movie stunt, my daughter's healing gifts probably prevented her from having to undergo surgery. Somehow, Joanie finds time to watch my debits and credits—and my back—to the immense relief of her very proud, very grateful dad.

It is my good fortune to experience demand for tens of thousands of my books each year. It is my doubly good fortune to have the distribution of those books handled with spooky accuracy and amazing speed by my son Mark. What makes his accomplishment all the more remarkable is that, like Joanie, he does this work part time. Mark is a brilliant portrait photographer, exceptionally artful at bringing corporate executives out of themselves for magazines, annual reports and marketing pieces. And he's photographed any number of high-profile people in film and theater. His portrait of a scowling Mickey Rooney—who got into a test of wills with Mark, and lost—is for me the most unique image ever made of a guy who's been a star for three quarters of a century. And Mark's sensitive portrait of his contemporary, the actor Jason Ritter, is the one that hangs in Jason's mother's home. If all this were not enough, Mark also designed the cover of this book.

Outside of our family, this book owes much to the perceptive and creative design of Laura Zavetz, and to the skillful care of the master printers of Alcom Printing.

ABOUT THE AUTHOR

©MARK MURRAY

NICK MURRAY WAS BORN IN THE BOR-
ough of Queens in the City of New York in
1943, and began his career in the financial advisory profession in 1967. In 1975, he was a
founding director of the New York City chapter
of the organization now known as the Financial
Planning Association.

Behavioral Investment Counseling is his tenth book for financial
services professionals since 1987. His only book for investors, *Simple Wealth, Inevitable Wealth,* is among the most successful pri-
vately published books of the last ten years.

Nick was the 2007 recipient of the Malcolm S. Forbes Public Aware-
ness Award for Excellence in Advancing Financial Understanding.